2
THE BUDGET IN THE AMERICAN COMMONWEALTHS

STUDIES IN HISTORY, ECONOMICS AND PUBLIC LAW

EDITED BY THE FACULTY OF POLITICAL SCIENCE OF
COLUMBIA UNIVERSITY

Volume XXV] [Number 2

THE BUDGET IN THE AMERICAN COMMONWEALTHS

BY

EUGENE E. AGGER

AMS Press, Inc.

New York

1967

AMS Press, Inc.
New York, N.Y. 10003
1967

Manufactured in the United States of America

PREFACE

In the preface to Professor Burgess's work on Political Science and Constitutional Law one reads the following words: "It is, indeed, a serious thing to ask the world to read a book. It should never be done unless the book answers a purpose not fulfilled, or not so well fulfilled by some book already existing." Ever since the author of this monograph read that statement his own conscience has been troubling him sorely. The need for some treatise on the subject with which this one purports to deal has been, of course, generally recognized; but whether the pages here offered meet this need to a degree that justifies their publication is a question concerning which the author has been harassed by numerous doubts. Now, however, it is too late to retract, and therefore the author fondly cherishes the hope that at least somebody may find something of interest somewhere within these pages, and if such person be only induced to go into the matter a little further, the author will feel that what he has attempted has not been entirely in vain nor absolutely without justification.

In the second place, the author desires to explain that in only a few cases has he been able to go into the court decisions, concerning certain points that are discussed in the body of the monograph. The reason for this was that he found that such decisions were entirely too numerous to permit an examination of them for all the states, as would have been necessary if he were going to attempt it at all. He hopes at a later time to work this out more fully.

Finally the author desires to acknowledge his gratitude to all those who in divers ways have helped him in the preparation of this monograph. Certain acknowledgments are made in the text and emphasis is laid upon them at this place, but it is to Professors Seligman and Seager of Columbia University that the author is most deeply indebted and it gives him the keenest pleasure to express to them his sincere appreciation and gratitude. The author is also indebted to officials in every state of the Union for the kindness with which they answered numerous questions concerning conditions and practices in their respective states and to them, without attempting to give a full list of their names, he expresses grateful acknowledgments. To the others,—friends at Columbia and elsewhere,—who have been of service to the author in manifold ways during the preparation of this monograph, he expresses again his sincere thanks, and he trusts that they may never want for the kind of friends that they have been to him.

EUGENE E. AGGER.

Columbia University, 1907.

TABLE OF CONTENTS

PAGE

CHAPTER I

THE BUDGET RIGHT IN THE AMERICAN COMMONWEALTHS

Constitutionalism and the budget right 15
No dramatic circumstances connected with the development in the commonwealths 16
I. The provisions of the general constitution.
    Republican form of government guaranteed..................... 17
    The implication of such guarantee............................ 18
    The distinction between the budget right and the exercise of that right 18
    The limitations placed by the federal constitution on the exercise of the right 18
II. Provisions in the state constitutions embodying the budget right.
    Taxes levied only by the people or their representatives 20
    All revenue bills to originate in popular branch of legislature..... 21
        This embraces appropriation as well as revenue measures 21
        This principle not very important in the states................. 22
        The practice in the states 23
    No money paid from the treasury except in pursuance of an appropriation made by law 24
    Complete and comprehensive report on income and expenditure .. 25
III. The restrictions on the exercise of the budget right.
    a. The nature of the restrictions on the legislature here and abroad. 26
    b. Restrictions relating to the legislative session 29
    c. Restrictions relating to the legislative procedure............... 30
    d. Restrictions relating to the levying of taxes..................... 33
    e. Restrictions relating to appropriations and expenditure 36
    f. Restrictions relating to public debt and public credit........... 38

CHAPTER II

THE PREPARATION OF THE BUDGET

Introduction.
    I. The differences between the American and European procedure..... 43

TABLE OF CONTENTS

	PAGE
II. The causes of the overshadowing of the executive branch of the government	44
a. Form of government	44
b. Absence of financial stress	44
c. Further causes in the states	44
(1) No office corresponding to the European finance minister	44
(2) The influence of the general property tax	45
III. The effect of this	45

Part I

THE BUDGET AS A REPORT

I. Prepared by state officer	45
II. The law regulating the contents	46
III. What a budget should show	47
The shortcomings in the states	48
a. No clear picture of fiscal operations	48
b. Estimates are unsatisfactory	49
c. Recommendations inadequate	50
IV. Conclusion.	
Budget as a report unsatisfactory	50
The system is at fault	50
a. No real control of estimates by fiscal officer	51
b. No constitutional right to defend estimates	53
c. Estimates made are disregarded	54
V. The unfavorable reaction on the fiscal officers	55
VI. Criticisms.	
Intelligent action for the future rendered difficult	56
Balance and equilibrium in the budget jeopardized	56
Extravagance stimulated	57
VII. The outcome in the future problematical	57

Part II

THE BUDGET AS A PROJECT OF LAW

I. The organization of the legislature	58
II. The financial committees	58
a. Their appointment in the senate and in the lower house	58
b. The number and character of the committees	59
c. The names of the committees	60
d. The duties of the committees	61
III. The preparation of fiscal legislation	62
a. The period for which the budget is provided	62
The session of the legislature	62
The relation of the budget to the fiscal year	63

TABLE OF CONTENTS

	PAGE
b. The determination of appropriations	67
c. The preparation of revenue bills	68
d. The efficiency of the committee system	70
Committee cannot accurately measure needs	70
Divided responsibility makes equilibrated budget impossible	70
e. The form of the budget as reported by the committee	70
(1) What the scheme of appropriations should embrace	71
The practice in the states	72
(2) Appropriation measures	73
(*a*) Constitutional restrictions	73
(*b*) General appropriation bills	76
(*c*) Separate large bills	77
(*d*) Appropriations by general statute	78
(*e*) Classification and itemization	78
(*f*) Regularity in form	80
(3) Form of the revenue bills	81

Conclusion.

CHAPTER III

THE VOTING OF THE BUDGET

I. The organization of the legislature.	
a. Comparison of American and foreign conditions	84
b. The examination of the budget on the floor of the house in the states	87
Right of way of revenue and appropriation measures	87
The right to amend	89
The vote	91
c. The bill in the senate	92
Procedure similar to that in the house	93
d. Conference committee	93
Final passage	94
II. The power of the governor.	
The veto power in the various states	95
The influence it may exert	96
III. The budget delayed.	
The carelessness in the states	97
IV. The appropriation period.	
a. Lack of importance of this question in the states	101
b. Constitutional provisions and practice	102
Comparison made between the appropriations in the states and those of the general government	102
c. Ordinary appropriations	103

	PAGE
d. Annual appropriations	104
e. Special appropriations	105

V. The discrepancies between the estimated and the executed budget.

    a. Discrepancies between estimated and actual revenue 106
        (1) Surplus 106
        (2) Deficit 106
            Means employed for meeting deficits 107
            Constitutional limitations of indebtedness for casual deficiencies 109
    b. Discrepancies between the estimated and the actual needs of one or more departments of the state 110
        Deficiencies alone need remedial action 110
        Means employed for overcoming deficiencies 110
            (1) Supplementary budgets 112
            (2) Deficiency bills 113
            (3) Administrative appropriations 113
            The extent to which these means are employed in the states 113

VI. Suggestions for the improvement of the budgetary practice in the states.

    (1) The increase of executive influence in the preparation 118
    (2) The centralization of responsibility within the legislature itself .. 120

CHAPTER IV

The Execution of the Budget

Introduction 123

Part I

COLLECTION OF REVENUE

Prefatory remarks 123
    I. The General Property Tax.
        (1) The general property tax on individuals 126
            (*a*) Assessment 126
            (*b*) Equalization 130
            (*c*) Determination of the tax 138
            (*d*) Collection 140
        (2) The tax on the property of miscellaneous corporations 144
            (*a*) Assessment 145
            (*b*) Equalization 147
            (*c*) Determination of the tax 147
            (*d*) Collection 148

	PAGE
(3) The tax on the property of certain special corporations	148
Banks and banking companies	148
(a) Assessment	149
(b) Equalization	150
(c) Determination of the tax	150
(d) Collection	150
Quasi-public corporations	151
(a) Assessment	152
(b) Equalization	162
(c) Determination of the tax	163
(d) Collection	164
(4) Critical remarks relating to the administration of the general property tax	165
II. Gross receipts and earnings taxes.	
(1) Administration	172
(2) Critical remarks	174
III. License Taxes.	
(1) Administration	175
IV. Inheritance Taxes.	
(1) Property liable	177
Theory in Louisiana	177
Excessive bequests to administrators	178
(2) Appraisement of the estate	178
Appointment of appraisers	178
Appeal from appraisers' decision	179
(3) Collection of the tax	179
When due	179
Discount allowed	180
Rate of interest charged	180
To which authorities paid	180
(4) Enforcing the payment of the tax	181
V. Other special kinds of taxes.	
(1) The stock-transfer tax	182
(2) The mortgage tax	183

Part II

CENTRALIZATION OF REVENUE

(1) Settlements	185
(2) Transfer of funds	185
(3) Enforcement of payments	188

Part III
SAFEKEEPING OF THE PUBLIC FUNDS

The depository system.
- (1) Kind of institutions employed 191
- (2) How they are chosen 191
- (3) The number 194
- (4) Security of funds deposited 195
- (5) Critical remarks 197

Part IV
DISBURSEMENT

- (1) The "ordinators" and "payers" in the states 199
- (2) The process employed 201

CHAPTER V
THE CONTROL OF THE BUDGET

- (1) What the question implies 203
- (2) On the side of collection 203
- (3) On the side of expenditure 203
- (4) The function of the "ordinator" 204
  - The effect of group representation in the legislature 204
  - Practice in England and the United States 205
- (5) The practice in the states 206
  - Examination of claims and payments 206
  - Nature of such examination 207
  - Critical remarks 209
- (6) The examination of books and accounts 210
- (7) Publicity 217

Conclusion 218

BIBLIOGRAPHICAL NOTE.

In the following pages general references are made to the laws of the several states. These references are for the most part to codes and session laws. When the year is given, as for instance, "Laws of New York, 1905," it indicates that the session laws of such year are referred to. In other cases where no indication to the contrary is given, and where the reference is a general one, as for instance, "Laws of New York," it indicates that the general code of laws is referred to. Such general references refer to the following codes of the states:

Alabama: Code of Alabama, 1896.
Arkansas: Sandels and Hill, "Digest of the Statutes of Arkansas," 1894.
California: Political Code of California. San Francisco, 1903 and 1905. (Edited by Jas. H. Deering and Walter S. Brann.)
Colorado: Annotated Statutes of the State of Colorado. Edited by J. Warner Mills, Denver, 1891, 1897, 1905.
Connecticut: Revised Laws of Connecticut. Hartford, 1902.
Delaware: Revised Statutes of Delaware, 1893.
Florida: Revised Code of Florida, 1892.
Georgia: Revised Statutes. Code of 1895. Supplement, 1901. Nashville, 1895 and 1901.
Idaho: Political Code of the State of Idaho, Boise, 1901.
Illinois: Revised Statutes of Illinois. Edited by Harvey B. Hurd, Chicago, 1903.
Indiana: Revised Statutes of Indiana. Compiled by Frank A. Horner. Lawyers' Coöperating Publishing Co., 1901.
Iowa: Annotated Code of Iowa. Edited by E. C. Ebersole, Des Moines, 1897. Supplement, 1902.
Kansas: General Statutes of Kansas. Edited by C. F. W. Dassler, Topeka, 1901.
Kentucky: The Kentucky Statutes. Prepared by John D. Carrol, Louisville, 1903.
Louisiana: Revised Laws of Louisiana. Compiled by Solomon Wolff, 1897 and 1904.
Maine: Revised Statutes of the State of Maine, Portland, 1904.
Maryland: Public Local Laws and Public General Law. Codified by John Prentiss Poe, Baltimore, 1888. Supplement, 1898 and 1904.
Massachusetts: Revised Laws of Massachusetts, Boston, 1902.
Michigan: The Compiled Laws of Michigan. Compiled by Lewis M. Miller, Lansing, 1899.
Minnesota: The General Statutes of the State of Minnesota, St. Paul, 1894.
Mississippi: Annotated Code of Mississippi. Prepared by Thompson, Dillard and Campbell, Nashville, 1892.

Missouri: The Revised Statutes of the State of Missouri, Jefferson City, 1899.
Montana: Code of Montana, Butte, 1895.
Nebraska: Compiled Statutes of 1881, with Amendments to 1901, Lincoln, 1901. "Cobbey's Code." Annotated Statutes of Nebraska, edited by J. E. Cobbey, Beatrice, Nebraska, 1903.
Nevada: Compiled Laws of Nevada, 1861 to 1900 inclusive. Compiled by Henry C. Cutting, Carson City, 1900.
New Hampshire: The Public Statutes of the State of New Hampshire, Concord, 1900.
New Jersey: General Statutes of New Jersey, Jersey City, 1896.
New York: General Laws of New York, Albany, 1900.
North Carolina: The Code of North Carolina, New York, 1883.
North Dakota: Revised Codes of North Dakota, Bismarck, 1899.
Ohio: The Annotated Revised Statutes of Ohio. Annotated by Clement Bates. Everett's Edition, Cincinnati, 1905.
Oregon: Codes and Statutes of Oregon. Edited by C. B. Bellinger and Wm. W. Cotton, San Francisco, 1902.
Pennsylvania: Digest of the Laws of Pennsylvania from 17co to 1894. Edited by Pepper and Lewis. Philadelphia, 1896. Supplement, 1903.
Rhode Island: General Laws of the State of Rhode Island and Providence Plantations, Providence, 1896.
South Carolina: Code of Laws of South Carolina, Columbus, S. C., 1902.
South Dakota: The Revised Codes of the State of South Dakota, Pierre, S. D., 1903.
Tennessee: Annotated Code of Tennessee. Edited by R. T. Shannon, Nashville, 1896. Supplement, 1904.
Texas: Revised Civil Statutes of the State of Texas. Austin, Texas, 1895.
Utah: Revised Statutes of Utah. Salt Lake City, 1898.
Vermont: Statutes of Vermont, Rutland, 1895.
Virginia: Code of Virginia as amended to adjournment of the General Assembly, 1904. Edited by John Garland Pollard, St. Paul, Minn., 1904.
Washington: Codes and Statutes of Washington. Edited by Richard A. Ballinger, Seattle and San Francisco, 1897. Mahan's Supplement, San Francisco, 1903.
West Virginia: Code of West Virginia. Compiled by John A. Warth, Charleston, W. Va., 1900.
Wisconsin: Statutes of Wisconsin. Edited by Sandborn and Berryman, Chicago, 1898.
Wyoming: Revised Statutes of Wyoming. Laramie, Wy., 1899.

CHAPTER I

THE BUDGET RIGHT IN THE AMERICAN COMMONWEALTHS

WRITERS on financial subjects have always taken a peculiar satisfaction in pointing out how almost all the great struggles in constitutional history have been more or less intimately connected with the question of budget right. Nor has the emphasis thus laid upon the control of the public purse been in any sense a false one. It may be true that if monarchs and potentates had exercised wisely the powers that were entrusted to them, the mere question of budget right would never have been made the subject of revolutionary contention. But in that event it would probably also be true that the world would never have seen constitutional struggles of any kind. It is because the rulers of the world failed to rule with wisdom and moderation that this fundamental principle of modern constitutionalism, namely that the right to vote the taxes and the expenditures of the state is inherent in the people who pay the taxes, came to be insisted upon even to the point of violence and bloodshed. Long, long ago it was recognized as a truism that "he who controls the finances of a state controls the nation's policy" and our forbears acted wisely when they held firmly to this ancient Teutonic principle of budget control. As Professor Henry C. Adams points out, " the extent to which this right is recognized may be regarded as one of the surest indications of the degree to which popular government is developed."[1] "Constitu-

[1] Henry C. Adams, *The Science of Finance*, New York, 1899, p. 109.

tionalism is the idea, budgets are the means by which that idea is realized."[1] This being so, it would seem to be difficult to overemphasize the importance of the rôle that this simple rule of financial control has played in the great drama of world progress and our financial publicists have not, in making this fact so prominent, overstepped the limits that a just regard for truth imposes.

The development of the budget right in the commonwealths of the United States, however, lacks the intense dramatic interest that great conflicts and bloody strifes have given to the development of the right in general history. In colonial days there were occasional struggles between the governors of the colonies and the representatives of the people,[2] but after independence was achieved, in a revolution that was itself based essentially upon the issue of budget right, the principle became too firmly established in the American mind and practice ever to need reinforcement or ever even to suggest to an ambitious executive that it might be attacked with success.

With the adoption of the Constitution of 1787 this cardinal principle of popular government was very naturally embodied in the fundamental law of the land. Others have already discussed the application of it in the affairs of the national government [3] and it is not presumed that anything remains to be added to that discussion in this place. There is, however, some need of speaking more particularly about the matter in connection with the various commonwealth or state governments.

[1] *The Science of Finance*, p. 116.
[2] See for instance, Wm. Z. Ripley, *The Financial History of Virginia*, New York, 1893, chap. v; and C. S. Bullock, *Finances of the United States 1775-1789*, University of Wisconsin Bulletin, 1895.
[3] See for instance, Ephraim D. Adams, *The Control of the Purse in the United States*, in the Kansas University Quarterly, vol. 2.

I. *THE PROVISIONS OF THE GENERAL CONSTITUTION:*

The Constitution of the United States says nothing about the form of the various commonwealth governments except in Art. IV, Sec. 4, according to which the general government guarantees to the states a republican form of government. But the Constitution does not itself define what shall be considered a republican form of government, although it is, perhaps, to be presumed that it means a government patterned, in a general way, after the central government. Concerning this point Professor Burgess says, " The qualities of representation, limitation, distribution of powers between independent departments, co-ordination of departments and election must be regarded as the essential elements of what is known as the republican form of government." [1]

Accepting then this definition of the republican form of government, the question with which we are concerned is, what does this constitutional guaranty imply as regards the budget right in the various states? According to the definition, the Constitution of the United States requires that the state governments be representative and that there be independent yet co-ordinate departments among which the various governmental powers are distributed, *viz.:* the legislative, the executive and the judicial. But as the levying of taxes and the appropriation of public moneys is everywhere regarded as a legislative function,[2] the exercise of

[1] John W. Burgess, *Political Science and Constitutional Law*, p. 153.

[2] Concerning taxation, Judge Cooley says: " The power of taxation is an incident of sovereignty, and is possessed by the government without being expressly conferred by the people. It is a legislative power; and when the people by their constitutions create a department of government upon which they confer the power to make laws, the power of taxation is conferred as part of the more general power." Thomas M. Cooley, LL. D., *A Treatise on the Law of Taxation*, Chicago, 1903, p. 71.
As the power to tax and the power to spend the money so derived

that function may be considered as essentially guaranteed to the legislative branch of the commonwealth governments. It may be said therefore that the Constitution of the United States guarantees to the people of the states that the budget right within each commonwealth or state shall be exercised only by the legislature elected by and representing the people.

But at this point it becomes necessary to call attention to the fact that there is essentially a distinction between the budget right and the exercise of that right. The right itself is lodged in the people, while the exercise of that right is of necessity vested in the " government." Yet the people can and do put certain limitations and restrictions on their governments in the exercise of the budget right. The full right is, of course, an incident of sovereignty, and because in the United States the people are sovereign they have put some limitations upon the exercise of their sovereign right by the governments which they have constituted. This distinction sets the financial operations of the state and the federal governments in a somewhat clearer light and the necessity of mentioning it here will become more and more apparent as the argument progresses.

Assuming that the Constitution of the United States guarantees to the people of the commonwealth that the budget right shall be exercised only by the commonwealth legislature, we find that the Constitution does, however, itself put certain limits on the exercise of this right. These limits extend, however, only in one direction; that is to say, they affect only the taxing power. In the field of appropriation or expenditure the commonwealth's power is practically unlimited,—although a state or a commonwealth cannot, of course, legally appropriate any money for a purpose

are necessarily correlative, the argument applies with equal force to the appropriation of the public moneys.

that is contrary to the Constitution or the laws of the United States. The restrictions on the taxing power are as follows: Art. I, Section X, p. 2, says, "No state shall, without the consent of Congress, lay any impost or duties on imports or exports, except what may be absolutely necessary for executing its inspection laws, and the net produce of all duties and imports laid by any state on imports or exports, shall be for the use of the Treasury of the United States; and all such laws shall be subject to the revision and the control of the Congress." Paragraph 3 also provides that "No state shall without the consent of the Congress lay any duty of tonnage . . . . . ." In these two sections are found all the expressed limitations of the commonwealth's taxing power that the constitution of the United States contains. The Courts have, however, added another, namely that the state may not tax the property of the United States or the instrumentalities of the general government. The following quotation from Professor Burgess's work sets forth the situation clearly. He says, after referring to the forbidden export and import, and tonnage duties; "So far as the express provisions of the constitution are concerned, the commonwealths may tax everything else, to any amount and in any manner they may deem proper. The Court, however, has decided that the commonwealth cannot tax the property of the United States and the instrumentalities of the general government, and that when both Congress and the commonwealths tax the same subject the general government has precedence and must be first satisfied."[1] It may be concluded then that, with exception of the limitations here referred to, the budget right in the several commonwealths is, so far as the general government is concerned, quite unrestrained.

[1] John W. Burgess, *Political Science and Constitutional Law*, p. 152.

Each state has a constitution of its own which is the fundamental law within its particular domain, and each of these constitutions provides more or less in detail just how the budget right that is vested in each commonwealth by the Constitution of the United States is to be exercised. Thus we find, in addition to the comparatively few provisions that embody the cardinal principles of budget right and that are contained in the constitutions of all states where constitutionalism exists, that there are also, as a rule, in the constitutions of the American states numerous other provisions which are restrictive in their nature. Some attention will now be given to these principles and restrictions.

II. PROVISIONS IN THE STATE CONSTITUTIONS EMBODYING THE BUDGET RIGHT:

Consideration will first be given to the application, in the various commonwealths, of those principles, which, as was stated above, are usually looked upon as representing, in their entirety, the embodiment of the budget right.

The first of these principles concerns the right to order the tax levies and demands that all taxes shall be levied only with the consent and by the authorization of the people or their accredited representatives. Yet in only eight of the states do we find this principle expressed in the written constitution.[1] The manner of expression is not always the same, but the same general idea is aimed at. Sec. 3 Art. IX of the constitution of Florida provides for instance, that " No tax shall be levied except by law." The Wyoming constitution on the other hand provides that, " No tax shall be imposed without the consent of the people or their authorized representatives."[2] But although we find the

[1] Florida, North Dakota, Ohio, Oregon, South Carolina, South Dakota, Washington, and Wyoming.
[2] Art. 1, sec. 28.

principle definitely expressed in only eight of the commonwealth constitutions, it does not imply that any other principle is recognized in the practice of the other states. On the contrary it is a principle that is everywhere accepted in the United States and is considered by Americans to be such a "self-evident truth" that thirty-seven states have not considered it necessary to embody it specifically in their written constitutions. Short shift would be made of any executive who tried to levy a tax on his own responsibility.

The second general principle is a sort of corollary of the first and provides that all revenue bills shall originate in the more popular branch of the legislative body. Stourm in his excellent work, " Le Budget "[1] discusses the working-out of this principle in the various foreign countries and more particularly in France. Almost every constitutional history of England will give some information about it in England, while Mr. Ephraim D. Adams's monograph on "The Control of the Purse in the United States "[2] discusses the same subject in connection with our own national government. Both M. Stourm and Mr. Adams point out that this principle has come to embrace appropriation bills as well as the bills passed only with the view of raising revenue. This was, of course, the logical and necessary implication. Of what avail would it be to say that such and such a tax could or could not be levied if the proceeds of any and all taxes might be spent in whatsoever way the executive saw fit? A mere granting of the right to levy constitutes a very small part of financial control. Appropriations and expenditure are so important that a direct control of them by the people is quite as necessary to a com-

[1] René Stourm, *Le Budget*, Paris, 1889.
[2] Ephraim D. Adams, *The Control of the Purse in the United States*, in Kansas University Quarterly, vol. 2.

plete control of taxation, as is the control of those measures which are intended to produce the revenue.

In the commonwealths, however, this principle has really little constitutional significance. The state senators are just as truly representatives of the people as are the members of the lower houses. They owe their offices to the direct election of the people and are therefore responsible to the people for their acts. The only difference between the senators and the members of the lower houses, is that there is a smaller number of senators and the basis of representation is thus a little larger. Then in some states the terms of the senators are longer than are those of the members of the lower house. At best, the question of popular control as between the lower houses and the senates is simply one of degree, and therefore the need for a constitutional enactment, vesting in the lower house the sole control over financial matters is, from a constitutional point of view, almost entirely imaginary.

It does not surprise us therefore to learn that, out of the forty-five states of the Union, only nineteen require that bills for raising revenue shall originate in the lower house, while in the constitutions of nineteen others it is specifically stated that any bill may originate in either house and having originated in one house may be amended in the other. Furthermore the constitutions of the remaining seven states contain no provision at all on the subject. The constitutions of Louisiana and Nebraska do, however, specifically require that appropriation bills shall originate in the lower house, although the Nebraska constitution is one of those in which the Senate is given the right to originate revenue bills. In general then it would seem true, that however important this principle may have seemed at the time of the adoption of the federal Constitution,[1] the people of the

[1] That this principle was of very great importance at the time of the

states, in the majority of cases, did not and do not now, consider it as one which needs to be carefully safeguarded in their commonwealth constitutions.

With these varying constitutional provisions we rather naturally expect to find a considerable variation in practice. And in this respect our expectations are realized. Yet the whole matter is of such comparatively little importance from both a constitutional and financial point of view that a very detailed consideration would not be justified. A few general statements may not, however, prove superfluous.

As a rule, it may be said, that, in those states where the constitution does not vest the lower house with the right to originate revenue bills, the upper house or the senate, does nevertheless concede the right when a strictly revenue measure is concerned. But as to bills in which the revenue received is only an incidental consideration, the senate is less obliging. Exceptions can of course be found to this generalization. In 1905 for instance, the Iowa Senate originated the bill which fixed the tax-rate for the fiscal period. And as regards appropriations it may be said that, as a rule, wherever the state legislature observes the custom of passing a general appropriation bill these bills originate in the lower house. Yet cases can be found where the senate has originated general appropriation bills that have met the approval of the lower house. This is not infrequently true in Tennessee. In not a few cases the bill making appropriations for legislative expenses is regularly a senate bill. Moreover the senate never hesitates to amend the house appropriation bills and sometimes goes to the length of substituting entirely new bills for them. Finally as regards

ratification of the federal constitution can be seen from Mr. Adams's discussion. Adams, *The Control of the Purse in the United States*, p. 181, in the Kansas University Quarterly, vol. 2.

the other incidental or special appropriation bills,—of which there are usually a great number,—the senates seldom hesitate to introduce these. In Connecticut most of the appropriation bills are senate bills, in other states, Kansas for instance, the number is about half and half as between the lower house and the senate, while in still others,—Mississippi for example,—there are only occasional senate bills.[1] Thus it is seen that from the point of view of actual practice as well as that of constitutional requirement, the principle that all money bills shall originate in the lower branch of the legislature, is not, in the states, one that is very seriously regarded.

Another principle which is supposed to safeguard the control of the public money in the hands of the people is the one requiring that no money shall be paid out of the public treasury except in pursuance of an appropriation by law and on the warrant of a proper officer. This principle is in some form or other incorporated in a great majority of the state constitutions. Yet it is not found in all of them. But despite this, it is not at all to be supposed that the state executive officers can in the state without such constitutional provision disburse the public moneys according to their own ideas. The fact is that the duties of the state officers,—with the governor as a limited exception,—are prescribed by the legislature and therefore, notwith-

[1] The procedure in New York is a typical instance of the American practice. The Assembly originates the three great appropriation bills, but they are always radically amended in the Senate. The Assembly regularly refuses to concur, and these bills in their final form are the result of a conference committee made up of the House Committee on Ways and Means and the Senate Committee on Finance. Incidental appropriation bills originate occasionally in the Senate as well as the Assembly. The Senate Committee on Taxation and Retrenchment originates revenue measures almost as often as does the same committee of the Assembly.

standing the lack of express constitutional requirements, the legislature itself can see to it that this very essential principle is observed. It goes without saying that this is, indeed, uniformly the case. Where the constitution does not provide that payments out of the treasury be made on the warrant of some specified officer, pursuant to an appropriation by law, the laws of the state which regulate the duties of the various state officers do so provide.

The last principle which may be considered fundamental to budget right is that which demands that a complete and comprehensive report be given to the representatives of the people, of all the receipts and expenditures of the state, for the period intervening since the last of such reports was made. Where the legislature meets annually the principle demands an annual report but where less frequent sessions are the custom, the report may be made biennially or triennially as the case may be. The principle implies also that the competent and responsible official shall submit with such report, some estimate, more or less detailed, of the amount of funds that will be required for the next period. This particular phase of the principle is however almost without significance in the United States, and as it comes up for discussion in the chapter on the " Preparation of the Budget," further consideration of it may be waived at this point. But most of the state constitutions specifically provide for a periodic report on the state finances to the state legislatures. Yet in the case of a considerable number the necessity of such reports was regarded as another one of those "self-evident truths" which needed no special mention. Moreover here again it becomes necessary to remember that the regulation of the duties of the state officers is a prerogative of the legislature, and thus the legislature itself can demand a report or make an investigation whenever it so desires.

As a matter of fact these reports from the state officers who are in any way concerned with the collection or disbursement of public money are universally required in the states. Almost uniformly also, they must be printed for more or less general distribution covering periods varying from three months to two years, with monthly statements, very often, between the longer and more detailed reports. Thus not only the people's representatives but the people themselves, generally, can keep informed about their state's financial affairs.

It is in these principles, expressed or implied, then, in the various commonwealth constitutions that the basis of budget right is found. Other less important provisions might be discussed but this is needless. The full control of the public purse by the people is so fundamental to our institutions that it is almost inconceivable that it should ever be successfully attacked. The American people realize that today they need not concern themselves with constitutional principles. These are established and accepted once for all. The aim now is toward more effective administration and control.

III. THE RESTRICTIONS ON THE EXERCISE OF THE BUDGET RIGHT:

(A) *Nature of the Restrictions:* The struggle of constitutionalism has been in general a struggle against the executive. Those principles which we have in mind when we speak of budget right are principles that limit the executive—that put him more effectively into the control of the popular branch of the government. But a mere glance at the constitutions of some of our commonwealths, will convince one that the people of our country fear little from the state executives and that they have, rather, an abiding distrust of their own elected representatives which has expressed itself in restrictions of a multiform variety. It is true that some other states have restrictions upon their legislatures,[1] but in these cases the restrictions represent the advantage that the executive power is still able to maintain, an advantage that the people have not yet been able to overcome. But in the American commonwealths where the people's power is absolute, such restrictions mean something altogether different. They mean practically that the people's elected representatives cannot always be trusted and that it is better to define pretty clearly some of the things that the legislature may not do. When it is considered that the older states originally had none of these restrictions and that they came to be embodied in subsequent constitutions as a result of bitter experience, such restrictions, taken as a whole, form a rather suggestive commentary on our particular kind of representative government.

It was pointed out above [2] that there is an essential distinction between the budget right and the exercise of that right. The right itself is an incident of sovereignty while the exercise of it is vested in the "government." In England and France where the parliaments represent the sovereign organization of the people the exercise of the budget right by the parliaments is quite unrestrained. Both in the field of revenue and in that of expenditure the action of parliament is final unless rescinded or modified by a subsequent parliament. But in Germany, as Professor Henry C. Adams points out,[3] there is not found this absolute power. "German jurists assert that the power of the Reichstag to withhold supplies is limited by the established institutions and principles of the empire." Then too in Germany the army supplies must be voted for a period of

[1] Germany for instance, see below.   [2] Page 18 *supra*.
[3] Adams, *Science of Finance*, p. 112.

seven years. But these restrictions that are placed upon the Reichstag represent restrictions upon the German people themselves. They are the relics of absolutism that still survive in Germany. In the United States we find that in both the general government and the various state governments, restrictions on the exercise of the budget right have been placed, but these restrictions are altogether different from those found in Germany. In our country they represent the preponderance of popular control. They are limits placed upon the activity of the representatives of the people, by the people themselves, instead of restraints that measure the extent to which the people are still under the authority of their executive.

The restrictions placed upon the states by the federal constitution have already been referred to, so that there is no need of mentioning them further here. We are concerned now with the further restrictions that the state constitutions impose.

These restrictions are of various kinds, in some cases having to do with even the minutiae of administration. It must not however be supposed that all the states impose all of the restrictions that may be referred to, nor even that any one state imposes all of them. Although there are a few states which impose most of them, as a general thing any particular restriction is found in comparatively few of the states. But they must be taken as a whole nevertheless and looked at in their entirety to appreciate their full significance, because they represent a tendency in the development of American state legislative practice and more particularly in American state financial practice. Therefore they may best be considered by arranging them into general classes or groups, as follows: restrictions relating to the legislative sessions; restrictions relating to legislative procedure; restrictions relating to the raising of revenue; restrictions relating to appropriations and expenditure; restrictions relating to the public debt and public credit.[1] These classes will be considered in turn.

(B) Restrictions Relating to the Legislative Session:

The British parliament can at any time, by law, regulate the time and duration of its meetings. The Congress of the United States also can decide this question for itself as long as it meets " at least once a year." Our forefathers took a peculiar satisfaction in the frequent meetings of their representatives. They believed that the representatives of the people could not meet too often. But in our states we find that this ardor has cooled, and indeed under the avalanche of legislation that the state legislatures regularly roll down upon us, in some states it has not only cooled but has congealed into impatience to such an extent that the legislature is now regarded as an unfortunately necessary evil.

Some of the older states still permit their legislatures to meet annually and yet there are but six that do so.[2] Thirty-eight states permit only biennial sessions, while one state, Alabama, goes even further and allows only quadrennial sessions. Mississippi in her latest constitution provided originally for quadrennial regular sessions, although midway between the regular sessions there was to be a special session at which only appropriation bills could be

[1] It is not contended that these classifications can be considered hard and fast, for it is easily possible that any particular restriction may be considered in one class as well as another. For instance, a limitation on the amount of money that can be raised by taxation in any one year, besides being a limitation relating to revenue is also essentially a limitation of expenditure, so that it might be considered in both classes. The object aimed at is simply to get a classification that will permit a fairly clear presentation.

[2] Massachusetts, New York, New Jersey, Georgia, Rhode Island, and South Carolina.

considered. But this provision was subsequently amended and the sessions are now to be regularly biennial. In all of the states the governors can, of course, call special sessions but at such sessions only those measures may be considered to which the governor in his proclamation refers. Furthermore in about half of the states we find some restriction concerning the length of the legislative session. Wyoming limits the regular session of its legislature to forty days, West Virginia to forty-five days, which however a two-thirds vote of both houses may extend. A considerable number of states allow only a sixty-day session,—although Virginia by a three-fifths vote of both houses permits a thirty-day extension. California, Nebraska, Rhode Island, Kansas and Tennessee without definitely limiting the term in this way, do limit the number of days for which a legislator will be paid—which amounts practically to the same thing. Some states also limit the duration of special sessions.[1]

(C) *Restrictions Relating to Legislative Procedure:*

The restrictions that are referred to in this class have to do with certain things which might be expected to be dealt with ordinarily in the rules of the respective legislatures themselves. In general they are aimed to prevent eleventh-hour raids on the treasury and otherwise careless and loose legislation that might be forced through without due consideration.

In some half dozen of the states we find, for instance, that no law can be passed except by bill. In no less than twenty-four states there is a specific provision also, that no law shall contain more than one subject which must be expressed in its title and that no bill shall be so amended during its passage through either house as to change its original

[1] Florida, Nevada, Utah, and Tennessee.

intent and purpose. Sometimes where this provision is found an expressed exception is made of the general appropriation bill, but where this is the case, the scope of the general appropriation bill itself is almost always rather carefully defined. And even in some states that have no provision limiting the scope of bills to single subjects, the scope of the general appropriation bill is more or less rigidly outlined. It is also provided in some cases that bills for salaries, etc., shall contain no provisions on any other subject.[1] In California the limitation of the scope of the appropriation bills is carried so far that no appropriation bill, except the general bill, may contain more than one item.

A rather common requirement also, is, that before being advanced to its final passage, every bill must first be referred to and examined and reported by a committee. This is an interesting provision because it translates into legal requirement what has long been the actual practice in all American legislative bodies. It is a frank recognition of the utility, and an unqualified acceptance, of the committee system, a system that some critics have been wont to decry.

There are restrictions of a somewhat different character relating to the quorum etc., when appropriation and revenue bills are up for consideration. In some states we find that for certain kinds of appropriation bills special votes are needed. Thus Arkansas and South Dakota, for instance, require that two-thirds of the members of each house must vote affirmatively for any appropriation other than for the public debt, expenses of government, schools and invasion, insurrection or war, before such appropriation can be validly made. Wisconsin requires a three-fifths attendance of the members of both houses for a quorum on revenue bills. Four states will allow no appropriation of money or any di-

[1] Florida, Illinois, Oregon, and West Virginia.

version of funds by resolution.[1] Illinois absolutely forbids any appropriation in any private law while Michigan, New York, and Rhode Island require an affirmative vote of two-thirds before such an appropriation can be made. Nebraska requires a similar two-thirds vote on all deficiency bills.

Finally, the other restrictions that may be logically considered in this class are those,—more or less common,—which are aimed to prevent the introduction and the rushing through of measures of various kinds in the closing days of the session. It is a matter of common knowledge how even yet in the closing days of the session, measures are sometimes " railroaded " through, that would never have passed in the form that they did had there been time for adequate consideration. Consequently in some of the states attempts have been made to mitigate this evil by constitutional provision.

Fourteen of the states have some provision of this kind although in no two of them are such provisions identical. Colorado and Michigan prevent the introduction of any new bill whatsoever after respectively, the thirtieth and the fiftieth day of the session. Mississippi and Texas have a similar prohibition covering the last three days of the session. Maryland and Washington both require a two-thirds vote of the house wherein a new bill is sought to be introduced in the last ten days of the session, before the same can be introduced. California has a similar provision covering the period after the fiftieth day of the session. In Minnesota during the last twenty days of the session, no new bill can be introduced without the governor's " consent," while in Nebraska no new bill can be introduced after the fortieth day of the session unless the governor " recommends " it.

[1] Illinois, Nebraska, Kansas, and Minnesota.

In some cases, however, these restrictions apply only to revenue and appropriation bills. Thus Mississippi will not allow either appropriation or revenue bills to be introduced during the last five days of the session. In Alabama a similar restriction applies only to revenue bills and in Louisiana only to appropriation bills. Three of the states, Montana, North Dakota and Wyoming, modify the restriction somewhat by making an exception of appropriation bills for the expenses of the government but in the other states where the restriction is found in modified form, a member who desires to introduce an appropriation bill, after the prescribed time, must first obtain the unanimous consent of the house of which he is a member and in which he seeks to introduce his bill.

(D) *Restrictions Relating to the Levying of Taxes:*

Restrictions may be of two kinds and may be spoken of as positive and negative restrictions. A provision demanding that a certain thing be done is a positive restriction while one that demands that a certain other thing be not done is a negative restriction. One is no less a restriction than the other because each represents a limitation upon the freedom of action.

It is necessary to refer to this here because in the various states that put restrictions upon the legislature in the exercise of the taxing power, some of these restrictions are found to be postive while others are found to be negative.

Probably the most important of all is a positive one. In seventeen states of the Union,—mostly the newer states,—is found a provision to the effect that the legislature must provide sufficient revenue for each fiscal year, to defray the estimated expenses of that year and,—as a rule also—any deficiency that may have been carried over from the previous year. The estimated expenses include, of course, either expressly or by implication interest on the state debt. This is a most interesting provision because, in a sense, it very explicitly incorporates into the law of the commonwealths a theory, that in other constitutional states, is recognized only in Germany, namely, that the legislature has not the right to refuse to grant supplies for the support of the " established institutions " of the state. It may be objected that a provision for the raising of revenue is not a provision for appropriating revenue. But such an objection would hardly hold because a clause demanding that revenue shall be provided for certain purposes, would in essence stultify itself unless it also implied that the revenue so raised had to be appropriated for the purposes specified. The courts have not, as yet, had to pass on this question and the probability is that they never will have to do so. Nevertheless the restriction itself is of exceeding interest and of not a little importance.

The other positive restrictions that might be referred to here are of a much less sweeping nature. They relate to levies for school purposes, particular kinds of taxes—such as poll taxes the proceeds of which are to be used for specified purposes, and to levies for the public debt. They are of minor importance and may be passed over without further mention.

The negative restrictions belonging to this class are, however, more numerous. The broadest of these is to be found in three Southern states, Texas, Louisiana and Georgia, where the general purposes for which alone the taxing power may be used are more or less particularly specified. In Georgia for instance the constitution provides that the power of taxation by the General Assembly shall be limited to the support of the state government and public institutions; educational purposes in the elementary branches of an English education only; to pay the interest and principal of the public debt; suppress insurrection, repel invasion and defend the state in time of war and to pension Confederate soldiers or their widows.[1] In the other two states there are analogous provisions.

Somewhat different in character are those restrictions relating to the tax rate. In some state constitutions the maximum annual tax rate is prescribed. In a few cases [2] this is an absolute maximum while in others certain extensions are possible or certain exceptions are made.[3] In three states—Colorado, Idaho and Utah—the rate depends upon the assessed valuation of the property in the state. As this assessed valuation increases to certain points the maximum tax rate decreases,—although in each of these three states a higher rate is permitted if the proposition to levy such a higher rate is favorably voted on by the qualified electors who in the preceding year have paid a property tax. The necessity of an increased rate will have to be very obvious before any such sanction will be accorded it! In the regulation of the tax rate the new constitution of Virginia shows a characteristic which probably no constitution of any other state, can equal. From 1902 until 1907—or for a period of five years the tax rate on property is fixed by the Constitution.[4] It may, however, be that the object of this provision was to force the legislature to try other sources of revenue because the constitution contemplates, after 1913, a segregation of the sources of state and local revenue.

The other restrictions that might be referred to in this

[1] Sec. 5882, Constitution of Georgia, found in the Revised Statutes of Georgia of 1895.
[2] Alabama, Florida, Louisiana, South Dakota, and Texas.
[3] Virginia and Wyoming.
[4] Art. xiii, sec. 189, Constitution of Virginia, 1902.

class relate to the sources and methods of taxation rather than the rate of the tax. The general property tax is provided for in the constitution of almost every state in the Union and the rules for assessment and exemption are more or less particularly prescribed. In three of the states [1] the principle according to which railways must be taxed is laid down while the constitution of Virginia, again in this instance, fixes also the rate of taxation.[2] In Minnesota certain of the railway tax laws must be submitted to and must receive the favorable vote of the people before they can become valid. But restrictions of this nature are not common and most of the states give their legislatures a wider latitude than do the states to which reference has been made.

(E) *Restrictions relating to Appropriations and Expenditures:*

A majority of the states abridge, in one way or another, the exercise of the appropriation right. The most common restriction of this class is one that relates to one of the fundamental principles in American polity,—namely the separation of church and state. About half of the states have a restriction of this kind. In some it takes the form of a broad prohibition against the appropriation of any money for religious purposes. In a number of others the prohibition extends only to appropriations for religious sects or societies while still others simply forbid any appropriation for sectarian schools. Oregon's provision is, however, the most severe for it expressly forbids appropriations even for the customary religious exercises in the Houses of the Legislature. Such a provision differs materially in spirit from the provisions of the old New England constitutions.

As a matter of fact however, no state in the Union makes

[1] Missouri, North Dakota, and Virginia.
[2] Art. xiii, sec. 176, 177, 178 and 179, Constitution of Virginia, 1902.

any appropriations for religions "sects" or for sectarian purposes, although in almost all the states there are certain religious exercises connected with the opening of the daily sessions of the legislature. Ohio has some "church lands," which were set aside for religious purposes according to the terms of the Symmes purchase and which represent a trust, but this is an instance which is probably unique in American history. The absolute separation of church and state as a principle at the bottom of our institutions, has never been seriously questioned by Americans and the fact that some of the states include some provision concerning it in their constitutions, simply gives to it an additional emphasis.

A few of the states have somewhat similar restrictions concerning appropriations for institutions of various kinds not under the immediate control of the states themselves.[1] Three of the states forbid such appropriations outright.[2] The other four make various exceptions—either by specifying certain excepted institutions or by allowing such appropriations if a two-thirds vote in both houses can be mustered in favor of them.

Five of the states have certain restrictions concerning appropriations for claims.[3] Florida and Ohio allow no money to be appropriated for any claim the subject matter of which is not provided for by existing laws, although Ohio makes an exception of such claims as two-thirds of the members elected to both houses will approve.[4] In the other three states the provision requires simply that the

[1] Alabama, California, Colorado, Louisiana, Pennsylvania, Virginia, and Wyoming.
[2] Colorado, Louisiana, and Wyoming.
[3] Florida, Ohio, Kentucky, Kansas, and Nevada.
[4] Art. ii, sec. 29, Constitution of Ohio.

claim shall not be recognized by the legislature unless it has been audited in the regular way.

Finally, corresponding to the provision prescribing a maximum tax rate, there are found in four of the states,[1] provisions forbidding the legislature to make appropriations beyond the revenue provided, unless the measure making such additional appropriations also provides an additional and sufficient tax to cover the appropriations so made. And where a maximum tax rate is prescribed there is also the provision that the aggregate tax rate shall not exceed the prescribed maximum. In these four states at least, " deficit financiering " is prohibited by law—but it must be conceded that the experiences which made it seem wise to the framers of the constitutions of these four states to include such prohibitions in the constitutions can hardly be said to have been such as scientific deficit financiering might afford! But it is doubtful whether the prohibitions are worth much after all. The revenue provided can be only estimated at best and nothing in the past gives any warrant to suppose that the legislatures would feel themselves very rigidly bound to observe such a provision even though they might, with relative accuracy, be able to estimate the revenue that was to become available for the period during which the appropriations were to run.

(F) *Restrictions Relating to Public Credit:*

In all but a few of the New England states there are found various restrictions that limit the extent to which and oftentimes the purposes for which the public credit may be employed. These restrictions represent, for the most part, the results of experience, either of the states themselves which now impose them or of other states which were taken as object lessons.

[1] Colorado, Idaho, Montana, and Utah.

Thirty-four states of the Union forbid the loaning of the state's credit to any individual or corporation,—although North Carolina and Rhode Island which are among these thirty-four will permit it in any particular case, if the people give their assent in an election held for the purpose. Twenty states forbid the subscription, on the part of the state, to the capital stock, etc., of any corporation or company. These provisions date, as a rule, from the late forties and early fifties when so many of the states entered into wild schemes of turnpike-road, canal and railroad building, from which comparatively few emerged without serious loss.

The most important of this class of restrictions, however, relate to the amounts and purposes of the public debt. Here are found all sorts of limitations ranging from absolute prohibition of all state indebtedness, except for war, invasion or insurrection, to the other extreme of practically no limitation whatsoever.

The most common provision is one which is made up of a series of distinct parts. In the first place it allows the legislature to contract indebtedness for casual deficiencies and extraordinary expenses although it limits to a specified amount the indebtedness that can be so incurred. In the second place it allows the contraction of indebtedness for any other purpose; but before the debt can be contracted, a law authorizing such a debt for a single purpose, must be passed; the law must provide for the establishment of a sinking-fund to pay the interest at stated times and to liquidate the principal within a prescribed period. The whole project must then be voted on by the people at a general election, and if at such election a prescribed majority votes in favor of the measure, then and only then, may the debt proposed be contracted. Furthermore it is provided that the money so raised can be used only for the purpose specified in the law, and the tax that is levied remains irrepealable until the debt, for which it was imposed, is liquidated. Eleven states[1] have clauses in their constitutions substantially to this effect although in one or two the provisions may not be so complete. The limit for deficiencies and extraordinary expenses varies from $1,000,000 in New York to $50,000 in Rhode Island. In Idaho and Wyoming the limit is a certain percentage of the assessed valuation of the property of the state. The period over which an additional special debt is allowed to run also varies greatly. One or two states allow this to be determined entirely by the legislature while the others give the maximum number of years during which the indebtedness may be outstanding. South Carolina fixes the maximum at forty years, New Jersey at thirty-five years, New York at eighteen years, Missouri at fifteen years and so on. Some also, require the interest to be paid semi-annually while in others simply an annual interest is called for. In all vital matters the direct control of the public credit is thus, in these states, lodged with a high degree of security, in the hands of the people themselves.

Next in degree of restrictions of this kind, come a number of states which prescribe a limit beyond which *all* state indebtedness may not go, but which do not limit to any particular purpose or purposes the objects for which such debts may be contracted. Five states have provisions to this effect.[2] In four of the states there is a rigid limit expressed in dollars, though it varies as between the states themselves. Oregon places a $50,000 limit while Maine and Nevada have fixed theirs at $300,000. In Wyoming, where the limit is 1% of the assessed valuation of the property in the state,

[1] California, Idaho, Illinois, Iowa, Kentucky, Missouri, New Jersey, New York, Rhode Island, South Carolina, and Washington.
[2] Maine, Nevada, Oregon, Utah, Wyoming.

the limit rises in proportion to the increased valuation of property. A few other states go a step further in this policy of restriction and not only limit the aggregate indebtedness, but also specify the purposes for which such indebtedness may be contracted, requiring in some cases that every debt be voted on by the people. Then in the last group, come Florida and Louisiana which absolutely prohibit all indebtedness except for insurrection, invasion and war.

From the above discussion it appears that the American people doubt the wisdom of vesting their representatives with the full exercise of the budget right. They demand for themselves the right to control directly the essentials of the state's financial policy and this demand has been expressed in the variety of restrictions that have been passed in review. Two states have pressed this demand so far that they have incorporated in their organic law the full system of initiative and referendum.[1] This is the highest development of the tendency toward popular interference with or control of the legislature.

In the foregoing survey of the constitutional provisions embodying the budget right and the constitutional restraints that have been placed upon the exercise of that right, it has not been attempted to bring to light all the minute details and distinctions that are to be found in the American states. An exhaustive description of existing conditions would require that almost every state be taken up separately. But such a procedure would be manifestly impracticable. The aim has been not to set forth the conditions in any one state particularly, but to show in a broad and general way the basis of the budget right in the commonwealths and how the exercise of that right is limited in this direction and in

[1] Oregon and South Dakota.

that by restrictive clauses in the various commonwealth constitutions which represent so fully the political liberty and the political convictions of the American people. It is the whole picture which is significant and too minute details must not be allowed to obscure it. In that picture can be traced not only the lines of hope and achievement but also those of disappointment and failure.

CHAPTER II

THE PREPARATION OF THE BUDGET

Introduction:

I. The American budgetary practice differs essentially from the European procedure in the relative insignificance of the part played by the executive in America and the all-dominant part taken by the legislature. Taking England as a basis of comparison—because English budgetary procedure is so far advanced—we find that in England every important measure introduced into the legislature must of necessity be a " government " measure. The preparation of the budget especially, is regarded as a government prerogative. If any material change were made by parliament in the budget as presented by the government, the whole ministry would resign. In the United States, however, the influence of the executive branch of the government is normally a very small one.[1] The recommendations of the executive officers are clothed with no particular authority but are taken for what they are worth in the legislative assemblies. Moreover, in the United States the preparation of the budget is regarded as the preparation of a law, and, indeed, as the preparation of quite the most important law with which the legislative body has to deal, and since lawmaking is the legislature's peculiar function it has uniformly safeguarded to itself the sacred prerogative of preparing the budget.

[1] Reference is made here not so much to the President of the United States or the Governors of the various states as to the other executive officers.

II. The causes of this overshadowing of the executive in the preparation of the budget are perhaps two-fold. In the first place our form of government has rendered it almost inevitable while in the second place our finances have never been in such a state as to render the practice dangerous. In the United States there is a rigid separation of the various powers of government among several distinct departments. Each department is naturally very jealous of its powers and as the danger lies in the encroachment of the executive on the legislative branch of the government, our American legislative assemblies have always been careful to check the growth of any custom that might abridge in any permanent manner what they loudly insist upon as their constitutional rights. Consequently no American legislative assembly has ever allowed the executive officers to exercise such a controlling influence in the formulation of the budget as is enjoyed by the executive officers in England.

In the second place, we have never for any considerable length of time been subject to a want of funds. In normal times financial stress has never been very acute. In our national government the problem that has usually confronted Congress has been how to get rid of the large surpluses that the tariff brought in. Consequently the need of a careful and economical administration of the finances has never been very pressing and the necessity of following the counsel of the administrative officer in charge of the finances has never been recognized.

In the state governments two further causes ought to be referred to in this connection. In the first place there is not in the state any officer corresponding to the European finance minister. In fact the financial operations of the states are not sufficiently important to require such an officer. In the states the chief auditing officer, and in some cases the state treasurer, exercises a supervising authority over the state's finances. But this involves no direct responsibility in any way similar to that attached to the Chancellor of the Exchequer or to that of even the Secretary of the Treasury, and it is obvious therefore, that the financial officer of a state is in no position very materially to influence legislation.

In the second place it must be remembered that the states depend, for the most part, on the general property tax for the bulk of their revenue. Whatever else may be said about the general property tax it cannot be gainsaid that its return is relatively certain and constant. By an easy adaptation of the rate the revenue needed can be supplied and it takes no very keen financial perception accurately to gauge the yield. This tends to diminish even more the dependence of the legislature upon the state's financial officer and allows the legislature to feel relatively free to prepare the budget according to its own ideas.

III. The effect of all this has been therefore that there is not in our country, especially in the states, the painstaking and careful preparation of the budget that characterizes the English practice, and in attempting to give a description of this practice in the states it will be necessary to consider separately the part played by the executive and that played by the legislature. Attention will be directed first to the budget as a report and in the second place to the budget as a project of law.

Part I

THE BUDGET AS A REPORT

I. *Preparation by State Officer:* The budget as a report is prepared by some official with a supervising authority over the state finances. It is usually the chief auditing officer—although in a few cases it is the governor and in others the treasurer. Such an officer is required by the constitution or by statute to prepare, for the use of the legislature, a more or less complete report on the financial condition and operations of the state. It is this report which must be considered as the budget in its first stage.

II. *The Law Regulating the Contents:* It is found that the law regulating the contents of such reports makes no distinction between the report that the chief auditing officer might be expected to make and that which might be expected from the officer charged with the preliminary preparation of the budget. The requirements relating to the finance officer's duties in one direction are mixed with those relating to his duties in the other direction.

These legal requirements vary considerably from state to state. In some states [1] the requirements are very comprehensive and definite; while in others [2] they are comparatively scant. In general however it may be said that what is required is a more or less detailed account of the receipts and disbursements of the state for the previous fiscal period, a statement of the public debt, estimates of the receipts and expenditures of the state for the subsequent period and general recommendations relative to the improvement of the state's fiscal system. In addition to these general provisions there are in almost every state, certain other special requirements and without attempting to specify just in what states each one of these may be found they may be enumerated about as follows: a full account of all claims audited; a full account of the taxes received and collected showing the amount yielded by each tax; an account of the appropriations that were made for the preceding period, the amounts expended and the balances in the treasury; a statement of the separate " funds "of the state; a statement of

[1] Arkansas, California and Nevada for instance.
[2] Maine or Florida for example.

the accounts of the states with the several counties; a statement of the assessed valuation of property in the state; an account of the taxes levied in the counties; a statement of the debts due the state; a statement of all claims against the state not provided for by law and a statement of all warrants issued, with the date of issue, to whom paid, for what purpose and under what law. As a rule also the officer making the report is supposed to include such other miscellaneous information as may appear to him to be worth imparting to the legislature. In no case are the legal provisions classified in a way that would indicate a clear perception of the difference between a mere auditor's report and a real budget.

III. *What a Budget should Show:* There are a variety of things which the budget as submitted by the executive to the legislature ought to show. It ought first to give a complete picture of the operation of the fiscal system during the previous period. The workings of the various revenue measures ought to be explained and the return from each carefully and clearly shown. On the side of expenditure the amounts expended by the various departments of the government and for the general purposes under each ought to be clearly set forth together with the appropriations that were provided for such purposes and the manner in which these have been applied. But even more important than this account of the actual workings of the system are the estimates of the receipts and expenditures for the coming fiscal period and the recommendations that are made to improve the fiscal system so that it may the more efficiently supply the revenues that are needed. It is here Stourm says, that the finance minister must show himself at his best.[1] Clearness, universality and sincerity are the high qualities that these

[1] *Le Budget,* p. 186.

estimates must possess. Do the budgets as reported by the responsible fiscal officers in the states meet these several requirements? It is perhaps unnecessary to say that they do not, and in view of the confused legal provisions referred to above, this is not to be wondered at.

(A) In the first place we cannot get a clear picture of the fiscal operations of the state for the period which the report is meant to cover. It will be found that occasionally individual officers will discuss more or less at length the workings of the revenue laws, but where so much depends necessarily upon the personality of the individual himself it is to be expected that, unless custom and tradition have enforced certain principles in this particular, there will be considerable variation in the reports of the various officers as one succeeds another. As a matter of fact this variation is characteristic. The report of one officer one year may contain a clear and illuminating discussion of the workings of the revenue laws, but in the very next year his successor may touch upon the subject in only a cursory way. In some reports indeed, there is no discussion of this kind whatsoever and the officers responsible simply introduce them with a few lines to the effect that the reports are submitted according to the requirements of law. Then the general tables which should show clearly the operations of the fiscal system during the preceding period are seldom found in such a shape that they give an accurate idea of such operations. There is no grouping in any adequate way, of the parts of the report that are really related to the budget and the parts that have no such relation. Almost twenty years ago Professor Seligman pointed out [1] some of the difficulties that are encountered by the student in trying to find out something about state finances from the state

[1] *Publications of the American Statistical Association*, vol. i.

finance reports. Practically the same difficulties are encountered today. In very few of the states has any improvement taken place so far as appears from a perusal of the later reports. The same system of accounting and the same loose practices still obtain and naturally the same confusion results. Professor Seligman did not criticise these reports from the point of view of the budget but to all intents and purposes his criticisms apply when the reports are so regarded.

(B) The estimates also are unsatisfactory. They too differ in character not only as between the reports in the various states but also as between those of successive officers in the same state. In some cases they cover but half a page and give simply the general heads of expenditure with the total amounts required. In other cases some attempt at particularization is made and the amounts required for the various purposes are given more in detail. In most cases the estimates of the revenue are on a net basis while both revenue and expenditure are estimated, as a rule, in general amounts or round numbers,—a fact which seems to indicate that what is aimed at is simply approximate accuracy.

In the preparation of these estimates various means of arriving at the amounts submitted are employed. When speaking of this in connection with other governments we usually refer to the "principle employed in the determination of the estimates;" but here we can speak of principles only by courtesy, because, so far as can be determined, the practice in our states is characterized by a lack, rather than by the employment, of any principle. In some cases the estimates are obviously little more than guesses. In other cases the officer responsible for the estimates simply communicates with the other officers, heads of departments, etc., obtains their estimates and includes them in his own without change. In a few cases he does consult these officers, etc., in person—" much to their disgust " writes the Treasurer of Vermont. In still other cases the practice is simply to take the appropriations that have been made for one period and to make them the basis of the estimates for the subsequent period. In New York for instance the Comptroller, Mr. Kelsey, stated that the many pages of estimates in his report constituted practically a transcript of the general appropriation bill of the previous year.

In no state have the estimates been found in such a form that they could be considered a complete and satisfactory basis for the budgetary legislation of the period for which they were intended.

(C) Recommendations for the improvement of the fiscal system are found in some of the reports but are entirely wanting in others. Where they are found they are sometimes comprehensive as well as clear and explicit, but it is probably fair to say that more often they are in the form of rather general suggestions. This general criticism would, however, not hold against the recommendations that are made to cure administrative defects in the existing laws. These usually seem very definite and to the point. The chief criticism, however, that must be brought against the reports from this point of view is one that applies not to the recommendations that are made but rather to the practice of so many of the states' fiscal officers of neglecting to make any recommendations whatsoever.

IV. *Conclusion:* Our conclusion must then be that in our states the budget as a report is on the whole very unsatisfactory. It is not to be supposed, however, that whatever blame this state of affairs implies is to be attached to the officers making the report. It is the system which is at fault and in the following section an attempt will be made to show why this is true.

(*A*) In the first place it must be remembered that the officer supposedly in charge of the finances of the state has in reality absolutely no authority or control over the estimates of the various officers, departments, etc., of the government. Placed as he is in a supervising capacity over the state treasury, observing where all the funds of the state go and for what purposes, understanding better than the legislators themselves the workings of the revenue laws, —because he has to enforce them while the lawmakers do no more than their name implies, — he better than anyone else is in a position to tell what additional strain the treasury can stand or in what particular it will have to be reinforced, and he better than anyone else is able to judge of the soundness and weight of the arguments of officers and heads of departments when they ask for increases in appropriations. He may however be as careful as he can be about his estimates, he may compute them as honestly and sincerely as the severest critic could demand, and yet all his labor will be of little avail. All the other officers know that if they want an increase in their appropriations it will not serve their purpose to consult the finance officer in the matter. They know that what he recommends does not count for very much. And in the same way the auditor, or whoever else is responsible for the estimates, is well aware of the fact that however much thought and care he may devote to the preparation of his estimates it is more than likely that his figures will be disregarded. Nowhere in the states does an auditor or a comptroller exercise any real control over the estimates, and nowhere do the heads of departments or of state institutions have to come to him for any increase that they may desire. The legislative determination is always independent and final and it is to the legislature itself rather than to the finance officer that those seeking appropriations go.

These facts are so well established that in several cases the various state officers are required to submit their estimates directly to the legislature, or if transmitted first to the finance officer they are included in his report without modification or change. Thus in Iowa and Wisconsin the Board of Control submits the estimates of the needs of the various state institutions directly to the legislature. In New York the State Superintendent of Public Instruction submits the estimates of school moneys, etc. and the Fiscal Supervisor of Public Charities submits estimates for the various state charitable organizations. In North Carolina both the auditor and the treasurer are required to submit complete sets of estimates.[1] In Massachusetts the officers and the boards are required annually to send to the auditor " estimates in detail and tabular form "[2] but these estimates are embodied without change by the auditor in his report to the legislature. In Connecticut alone do the laws give the finance officer any semblance of authority over estimates. In Connecticut the Treasurer in connection with the Secretary of State, prescribes the rule according to which all estimates must be itemized. The law requires that for each department, etc., a specified officer shall prepare the estimates and submit them to the Treasurer according to the form prescribed by him and the Secretary of State. It is further required that whenever any material increase or variation of expenditure of the previous year shall be made the person responsible must give the reasons.[3] This gives the Treasurer an opportunity to combat the " reasons " or the arguments advanced and materially enhances his influence,

[1] Laws of North Carolina, vol. 2, ch. 44, sec. 3350, and vol. 2, ch. 23, sec. 2864.
[2] Laws of Massachusetts, 1905, ch. 6.
[3] Revised Statutes of Connecticut, sec. 62 and sec. 63.

but unless a serious oversight has been committed it may be said that Connecticut stands—in this particular—alone.

The practical worthlessness of the estimates submitted by the finance officer is of course generally recognized, and where they are still required it is merely because that is the usual custom or because of some other reason of similar significance. In some states the situation is squarely met and the officer responsible is relieved of the duty of submitting any estimates at all.[1] It was as recently as 1904 at the present Comptroller's own suggestion that the legislature of New York amended the law regulating the duties of the Comptroller so that now the usual estimates of receipts and expenditures are not required to be submitted in his report. When questioned about this the Comptroller stated that the several pages of estimates were simply so much "padding" in his report and declared that the only one who obtained any benefit from them was the state printer.

(B) In the second place the finance officer has no constitutional right to defend his estimates before the legislature; that is to say, after once the estimates have left his hands his authority over them—such as it was—ceases. He may or may not go before the legislative committee and urge their acceptance but whether he does or not depends upon the individual. In Connecticut the information is vouchsafed that "it is customary" for the treasurer to appear before the legislative committee. The present auditor of Delaware writes that he has done so but so far as he knows none of his predecessors in office did. The Missouri auditor writes that it is the usual practice of the auditor to appear before the committee not so much to urge the ac-

---

[1] New Hampshire, New York, and Tennessee. In New Hampshire, however, most of the appropriations are permanently provided for.

ceptance of the estimates as to explain them. The North Dakota auditor claims that he is " never asked " to appear before the Committee and consequently he does not do so. The Virginia auditor says that if the committees need an " explanation " from him they send for him and he adds also, " I have no voice in legislation so I do not volunteer my opinion." Thus it is seen that the practice in this particular varies from state to state and often from time to time in the same state. The constitutional standing of the finance officer before the committee is, however, in no sense different from that of any other individual who may ask to be heard.

(C) In the third place the finance officer soon learns that however conscientious and painstaking he may be, his recommendations are disregarded. His seemingly preeminent position in being able to determine accurately what the estimates should be is not recognized. There is a complacent self-sufficiency about the normal legislator which defies attack. He admits only with painful reluctance that anybody has qualifications superior to his own to judge of the essential wisdom of any particular course of action and especially in the matter of appropriations the idea that a mere official should have more authority than he is utterly repugnant and offensive to him. Therefore he will never consent to bind himself to the finance officer's estimate and almost uniformly certain considerations make it seem advisable to him to depart from them.

Moreover, the recommendations that the finance officer makes for the improvement of the revenue system are also treated, as a rule, with but scant courtesy. If such an officer be a strong man personally and one of the party leaders, he may exert considerable influence but the mere office that he holds will avail him little. And yet, presumably at least, he is in an especially good position to tell of the practicability and efficacy of any particular measure and the advice that he gives might be expected to be sound. But as a rule his advice shares the fate of all good advice. In Germany and Japan, it is said, expert advice is accepted because it is expert advice, but in America we reject it for the same reason. In Alabama, it is true, the Governor, Auditor and Attorney General, before each regular session must prepare a general revenue bill which must be presented to the legislature, but the law distinctly specifies that this is only for the legislature's " information," and in North Carolina also it is the duty of the treasurer to present in addition to the estimates of the state expenses, " a scheme in the form of a complete revenue bill to sustain such estimates." [1] A dozen examples could however be adduced to show that our state legislatures, as a rule, pay no attention to the " plans and recommendations " which they require from the finance officer. One example is given here that was chosen for its moderation. It is found in the report of the Auditor of Nebraska: " My predecessors in office for a number of years past have called attention to the gradually increasing debt of the state and a necessity for a revision of the revenue laws. Recommendations made have passed unheeded by successive legislatures." [2] Every one who has had occasion to read over reports of the state auditors and comptrollers will remember how often similar statements are found. No state finance officer can be said to be even remotely responsible for the state's fiscal system.

V. *Unfavorable Reaction:* The absence of any real authority over the estimates, the inability adequately to defend the estimates that are submitted and the disregard which is accorded the recommendations when presented to the legislature have reacted unfavorably upon the finance offi-

[1] Laws of North Carolina, vol. 2, ch. 23, sec. 2864.
[2] Report of 1902, p. 51.

cers in the states. When a large measure of control is given and an officer is held accountable for the showing that is made, his very self-interest will demand that he conduct his office in the most efficient way and that he present the result of his administration with thoroughness, clearness and accuracy. But it has been indicated that nowhere in the states does a finance officer exercise any real financial control. In the matter of estimates for instance, he knows that however much care and forethought he may devote to their preparation, the results of his labor are almost sure to be disregarded. Very naturally he asks himself the use of wasting time and thought on such a task—because in reality there is no use of doing so—and he therefore prepares his estimates in a perfunctory way simply to obey the law. This in fact characterizes his habitual attitude and accounts in large measure for the insignificance of the budget as a report in the states. Where no responsibility is given it cannot be expected that any will be felt.

VI. *Criticisms:* The criticisms that are to be made against the practice as thus established are entirely financial in character. An inadequate report on the operations of the fiscal system means that its workings will not be entirely understood and that intelligent action for the future is rendered correspondingly difficult. The failure of the legislature to obtain complete and carefully prepared estimates of receipts and appropriations makes it probable that the scheme of expenditures will not be as efficient as it might have been and that the adaptation of the revenue system will be faulty. In other words balance and equilibrium will probably be wanting in the budget. This is indeed uniformly the case in the states. In the last place the failure to follow the counsels of the finance officer may lead to ill-advised legislation—or perhaps to a failure to prepare for emergencies in due season and to consequent disaster. In general, also, loose practices stimulate carelessness and extravagance not only on the part of officials but also on the part of the legislature itself. These are qualities for which, indeed, most of our state legislatures have been consistently distinguished.

VII. *The Future:* What the outcome may be is somewhat problematical. The great development of municipal activity and the resultant increase in municipal expenditure in this direction and in that, have forced the cities into a budgetary practice that approximates the theoretical requirements much more nearly than does the practice in the states.[1] The state legislatures have imposed a sound system upon the cities but unfortunately there is no power which can impose it on the states themselves. Furthermore it is not likely that the activities of the state governments will develop so rapidly and extensively as have municipal activities and consequently the need of economical administration may never be felt. Nevertheless the development of the tendency toward the segregation of the sources of the state and local revenue,—a tendency which is giving the state the changeable and less certain sources—will require a much keener financial perception for the successful administration of the states' finances than has the relatively simple system of the past. This ought to bring the officer at the head of the finances of the state into more prominence and ought materially to enhance his influence and authority.[2]

[1] See *A Comparative Study of the Administration of City Finance in the United States*, by Fred. R. Clow, Ph. D., in Publications of the American Economic Associations, 3d series, vol. 2, no. 4.

[2] Something of this kind has already manifested itself in New York. The author was informed that the Comptroller's office had much to do with the passage of the Stock Transfer Tax Act and the Mortgage Tax Act, which latter, however, has since been repealed and replaced by a recording tax.

Part II

THE BUDGET AS A PROJECT OF LAW

I. *THE ORGANIZATION OF THE LEGISLATURE:*

In Part I an attempt was made to show that the rôle played by the executive in the preparation of the budget is relatively insignificant. Budgetary procedure in the states begins in reality with the legislature. It is obvious however that the legislature as a whole is too unwieldy a body efficiently to prepare the budget, and, as a matter of fact, this important task is everywhere delegated to a special committee. It is indeed characteristic of our entire legislative procedure that a large part of the preparation of laws is done by committees. An account of the development of the committee system would therefore be valuable, but here we may take into account only those things that are immediately relevant and the discussion must confine itself to the financial committees and their organization and methods. It is these financial committees which are in reality the finance ministers of the states.

II. *THE FINANCIAL COMMITTEES:*

(A) *The appointment of the committees* in each state is provided for by the rules of the legislatures. The method employed by the lower house usually differs from that employed in the senate. In the lower house the Speaker is given a relatively free rein in the appointment of members to committees. In the senate however, because the presiding officer is the lieutenant-governor, the committee assignments are arranged by the party leaders although in some states the president of the senate has nominally the appointing power. Where the president of the senate does not possess this power the committees are elected by the senate itself.

In all cases full party-representation is provided for. It is to be expected, of course, that the Speaker in the lower house and the majority leader in the senate will arrange the committee assignments of the majority in such a way that on the whole, the majority representation on each committee will be as strong as possible. This is uniformly the case. It might also be supposed that in arranging the minority assignments those in power would do their best so to scatter the forces of the minority that, on the whole, the minority representation on each committee would be as weak as possible. But fortunately party advantage is never pushed to this extreme and the general custom is for the Speaker to take the minority leader's counsel in the committee appointments of the minority. In the senate also the minority leader is responsible for the committee assignments of his followers. In general then the organization of the committees in both the senate and the lower house is based upon considerations of party advantage; but as each party is desirous of making the best possible showing before the people, party advantage itself demands that ability and fitness be taken very largely into account in the selection of the members to serve on the various committees. In this particular then, the pressing of party advantage redounds in the long run, to the people's benefit.

(B) *The number and character of the financial committees* differ from state to state. The common practice is to have one committee in general charge of appropriations and another in charge of measures for raising revenue. In some states both functions are united in one committee.[1] In a few states this characterizes the senate committees only.[2] A few other states have joint committees of the

[1] This is true in Arkansas, Idaho, Indiana, Maryland, Rhode Island, South Carolina, Tennessee, Vermont and West Virginia.
[2] Delaware, Montana, and New Hampshire.

lower house and the senate—one for appropriations and one for revenue.[1] Then there are as a rule other committees for special purposes or special kinds of measures such as the Committee on Excise in New York.

(*C*) *The names of these committees* also differ very much from state to state. The committees of the lower houses in charge of appropriations are variously known as committees on "Ways and Means," or on "Appropriations" or on "Finance." Committee on Appropriations is the most common designation. There is a much wider variation in the names of the committees in charge of the revenue measures. "Ways and Means" is the most common, "Revenue and Taxation" follows next in order but all the following names can be found: Ways and Means and Revenue; Assessment and Collection of Taxes; Retrenchment and Economy; Finance; Taxation; Assessment and Taxation; Revenue, Finance and Taxation; Taxation and Retrenchment; and Taxes, Ways and Means. In New Jersey the Committee on the Judiciary and in Kansas the Committee on State Affairs have charge of revenue measures in their respective states. In a great many of the states the names of the committees in the senate are the same as those in the lower house. Where both the revenue and the appropriation functions are united in one committee the following names may be found: Ways and Means; Finance; Appropriations; Taxation and Finance; and Finance, Ways and Means in the lower houses: and Finance, Taxation and Finance; Finance, Ways and Means in the senates. The names of the joint committees are as follows: (for appropriations) Joint Committee on Claims,[2] Joint Committee on Appropriation and Financial

[1] Wisconsin, Maine and Connecticut.
[2] Wisconsin.

Affairs[1] and Joint Committee on Appropriations;[2] (for revenue measures), Joint Committee on Taxation,[1] and Joint Committee on Finance.[2]

(D) *The duties of these committees* are sometimes prescribed by the rules although in their fullness they are determined by custom. The committees must study the measures that are submitted to them and they have also the power to initiate legislation connected with their particular fields. Almost all the important fiscal legislation originates in the committees.

The committee that has general charge of appropriations uniformly originates the bill-making appropriations for the expenses of the government,—where it is customary to pass such a bill,—but almost every committee has a right to report a bill carrying an appropriation for some purpose that directly concerns the field of the committee's responsibility and individual members of the legislature may introduce appropriation bills for specific purposes. It is, however, the general practice in the states to refer such measures to the committee in charge of appropriations before final action is taken on the floor of the house. There are, however, some exceptions to the general rule. In Florida it is not always done. In Vermont bills not carrying appropriations for the support of the government are not regularly sent to the appropriation committee. In Arkansas there is a division of responsibility resembling somewhat the congressional plan. The Committee on Ways and Means reports general appropriations; to the Committee on Charitable Institutions are referred all bills carrying appropriations for charitable institutions; appropriation bills for the university go to the Committee on the University and for the schools to the Committee on Schools.

[1] Maine.   [2] Connecticut.

In the same way all revenue measures go, as a rule, to the regular revenue committee although the important revenue measures originate in the revenue committees themselves. When bills are introduced by individuals or committees other than the revenue committees the revenue provided by such measures is usually only an incidental consideration.

There is thus in the state legislatures some centralization in the control of the two great classes of fiscal legislation. This centralization is highest in the states where a single committee in either house has charge of both revenues and expenditures and is on a somewhat lower plane, where there are independent committees for such purposes. The whole history of the committee system shows however that the tendency is away from, rather than toward, centralization. It was only in 1905 that Vermont provided for a separate revenue committee while before that time one committee had charge of both appropriations and revenue measures.

III. THE PREPARATION OF FISCAL LEGISLATION:

(A) The Period for which the Budget is provided: In the great majority of states the legislative sessions are biennial. In Alabama they are quadrennial. In only six states are the sessions annual.[1] This means that in all but these six states the revenue system must remain undisturbed for two or four years as the case may be; only in the six states which have annual legislative sessions can there be an annual budget.[2] From a strictly financial

[1] Massachusetts, Rhode Island, New York, New Jersey, South Carolina and Georgia.

[2] The practice in Georgia is very irregular. Sometimes the budget is voted for a year — sometimes for two years. There were, for instance, no general appropriation and general tax acts in 1901 but

point of view the general practice of having only biennial or quadrennial legislative sessions is one that is subject to some criticism in view of the fact that executive and administrative discretion is so narrowly restricted. It is usually considered difficult enough to forecast conditions for a year lying in the immediate future and this difficulty increases in geometrical progression as one goes farther and farther into the future. Consequently if careful financiering were required, it would be very difficult to prepare accurate estimates for the second year of the legislative biennium and practically impossible to do so for a third or a fourth year as would have to be done in Alabama.

There are, however, certain ameliorating circumstances which have been referred to before. In the first place the financial pressure in our states has never been really great; in the second place the activities of the average American state are relatively few and unchangeable, and in the third place the return from the property tax—which is the mainstay of state finance—is not subject to any considerable variation. These circumstances tend to weaken the financial considerations opposed to biennial sessions and such considerations are therefore easily counterbalanced by those in favor of restricted sessions.

The next point that naturally suggests itself is the relation of the preparation of the budget to the fiscal year. The accepted theory is that in order that the budget may be prepared with accuracy the fiscal year should begin as soon as possible after the close of the legislative session. The longer the period that intervenes between the preparation of the budget and the time it goes into effect, the greater is

there were in 1902 to cover the years 1903 and 1904. There were none in 1903 but there was a general appropriation act in 1904 to cover deficiencies for 1904 and for the whole of 1905. Then in 1905 there were again the general acts for two fiscal years 1906 and 1907.

the likelihood that unforeseen exigencies will overturn the original estimates. In forty-one states the legislatures meet early in January. In the other four states they meet at some other time.[1] In some states the legislature does not convene until after the opening of the fiscal year. In nine of the states whose legislatures meet in January, the fiscal year begins either January 1st or shortly thereafter so that in these states the opening of the legislative session and the beginning of the fiscal year are practically synchronous.[2] In eight states the opening of the fiscal year comes at an even earlier period than January 1st.[3] It is necessary to say, however, that in three of these states [4] there are practically independent appropriation years. In Ohio, instead of making appropriations for the fiscal years outright the appropriations are so made that the appropriation period takes in three-fourths of one fiscal year and one-fourth of the next. The appropriations are made in this way for two years so that in the year when the legislature meets, appropriations are available until one-fourth of the then-current fiscal year has elapsed. In Tennessee and Nebraska the appropriations are made simply for a specified period, the opening and closing dates of which have no regular relation to the opening and closing of the fiscal year.[5] These three states,

[1] Georgia in June, Louisiana in May, Florida in April, and Vermont in October.

[2] This is true in Delaware, Idaho, Maine, Missouri, Nevada, Rhode Island, South Carolina, Utah and Oregon.

[3] December 1st for Colorado, Massachusetts, Montana and Nebraska; November 16th for Ohio, and October 1st for Alabama, Tennessee and West Virginia.

[4] Ohio, Nebraska and Tennessee.

[5] The appropriation years in these states end as follows: February 15th in Ohio; March 31st in Nebraska, and March 19th in Tennessee.

then, ought in reality to be classed with those which will be referred to subsequently, but in all the others heretofore mentioned—since in them the budget is not prepared until after the opening of the first fiscal year of the biennium for which it is to provide—the conditions ought to be gauged with relative accuracy.

In all the other states whose legislatures meet in January the opening of the fiscal year comes after the legislature has convened. In over half of these states the legislative session is restricted variously from forty to ninety days.

TABLE I.

STATES.	Session of Legislature Begins.	Session Restricted To.	Date of Fiscal Year.	Suggested date of Fiscal Year.
Arkansas	January.	60 days.	April 1st.	
California	"	Pay for only 60 days.	July 1st.	April 1st.
Connecticut	"	....	Oct. 1st.	July 1st.
Illinois	"	....	Oct. 1st.	July 1st.
Indiana	"	61 days.	Nov. 1st.	April 1st.
Iowa	"	....	July 1st.	
Kansas	"	Pay for only 50 days.	July 1st.	March 1st.
Kentucky	"	60 days.	July 1st.	April 1st.
Maryland	"	90 days.	Oct. 1st.	May 1st.
Michigan	"	....	July 1st.	
Minnesota	"	90 days.	Aug. 1st.	May 1st.
Mississippi	"	....	Oct. 1st.	July 1st.
New Hampshire	"	....	June 1st.	
New Jersey	"	....	Nov. 1st.	July 1st.
New York	"	....	Oct. 1st.	July 1st.
North Carolina	"	60 days.	Dec. 1st.	April 1st.
North Dakota	"	60 days.	July 1st.	April 1st.
Pennsylvania	"	....	June 1st.	
South Dakota	"	60 days.	July 1st.	April 1st.
Texas	"	....	Sept. 1st.	July 1st.
Virginia	"	60 days.	Mar. 1st.	
Washington	"	60 days.	April 1st.	
Wisconsin	"	....	July 1st.	
Wyoming	"	40 days.	Mar. 31st.	

A glance at the above table will show that in Arkansas, Virginia, Washington and Wyoming,—states where the legislative session is restricted—the date of the fiscal year is—according to the rule referred to above—well placed. In the other states where also the legislative session is restricted, the rule would seem to demand that the opening of the fiscal year be advanced somewhat,—approximately to the dates suggested in the table. In the states which put no restrictions upon the sessions of their legislatures it becomes necessary to take into account the actual practice of the legislatures in regard to the time of final adjournment. It may be said that although the sessions run occasionally into June they practically never run into July. June 1st or July 1st would therefore suggest itself as the best date for the opening of the fiscal year. A glance at the table will show that five of the states have adopted one or the other of these dates. The others have later dates—as is indicated in the table—and these therefore might with advantage shift the opening of their fiscal years to the times suggested. In the four states whose legislatures meet at some time other than January, it is shown in Table II that the legislative session is restricted in three of them. In one of these

TABLE II.

States.	Sesion Begins.	Session Restricted.	Fiscal Year.	Suggested Fiscal Year.
Florida	April.	60 days.	July 1st.	July 1st.
Georgia [1]	June.	50 days.	Jan. 1st.	Aug. 1st.
Louisiana.......	May.	60 days.	July 1st.	July 1st.
Vermont	October.	....	July 1st.	Jan. 1st.

[1] The Georgia legislature met formerly in October. The Governor opposed the change which was made in 1905 but the law providing for it was passed over his veto.

states—Georgia—it might seem advisable to make a change. January 1st is suggested for Vermont although it was only recently that Vermont changed the opening of her fiscal year from December 1st to July 1st.

It must, however, be remembered that in four of the states [1] to which reference has been made above, comparatively few appropriations are re-enacted each session. In these states, with practically permanent appropriations, it matters very little when the opening or the closing of the fiscal year takes place. Furthermore the considerations that were advanced as modifying the criticism, from a financial point of view, of biennial and quadrennial legislative sessions, apply here as well, although to the extent that the criticism is a just one concerning the sessions, it becomes even weightier when applied to the fiscal year. That is to say, if it is just to criticise the practice of biennial sessions because such a practice makes accurate estimates for the second year exceedingly difficult, then there is even more justification for criticising the practice of having the opening of the fiscal year begin some five or six months after the close of the legislative session because such a practice simply increases the difficulty of rendering accurate estimates.

(B) *How the Committees determine the Amounts of the Appropriations:*

In preparing the appropriation bills the committee concerned has full power. It may or may not endeavor seriously to base its action on the recommendations of the finance officer. The various officers of the state and those wanting either increased or renewed appropriations write directly to the committee and endeavor in this way to press their requests; or they appear in person and by personal suasion attempt to bring about favorable

[1] New Hampshire, North Carolina, North Dakota, and Wisconsin.

action. Sometimes also members of the legislative body—not themselves on the committee but possessing some influence—are appealed to in order that they may bring their influence to bear in favor of the appellant. On the other hand, only a few of the finance officers who prepare the estimates aver that they themselves appear before the committee to defend and urge the acceptance of the estimates that they have made. Considerations of financial expediency are thus apt to be under-emphasized.

Nevertheless, the committee in preparing the appropriation bills is dependent very largely on the auditor's or comptroller's office,—as the case may be,—and must as a rule keep in pretty close communication with it. In considering the amount to be allowed to any officer or department the committee must know how much such officer or department was given before and in just what way such allowance was spent. Then too the committee must have in mind the probable amount of revenue that can be wisely raised. This requires a frequent reference to the records in the auditor's or comptroller's office and consultation with such official himself. Thus in an indirect way the finance officer may after all, exert some influence in the allotment of appropriations but it is an influence that depends upon the individual himself and the confidence he may inspire rather than upon any constitutional prerogative which he enjoys.

After the various parties interested have been heard the committee brings in its recommendations in the form of a bill that is reported as any other bill would be, and the measure is then ready for the consideration of the legislature. Its career in the legislature will be dealt with in the next chapter.

(*C*) *The Preparation of the Revenue Bills:*
Where revenue bills are regularly passed the pro-

cedure in formulating them is much the same as in the case of appropriation bills. The committee responsible must study carefully the workings of the revenue laws and this necessitates a close study of the auditor's or comptroller's report as well as of the reports of other officers or boards who are charged in any way with the administration of such laws. The amount of revenue required must be carefully estimated in order that adequate means of raising it may be supplied. Where one committee has charge of both appropriations and revenue, the task here referred to is not a difficult one, but where there is a separate appropriation committee or more than one, the difficulty increases materially. Such consultation as is had between the appropriation and the revenue committees is only informal and amounts usually to a personal consultation between the respective chairmen. A carefully equilibrated budget is therefore practically out of the question. The committee after settling on the amount of revenue that will be necessary brings in a bill providing for the amount determined.

In considering new legislation whether introduced by individuals and referred to the committee or initiated by the committee itself,—the committee gives all parties interested an opportunity to be heard. A public hearing on the bill is usually announced and those interested one way or another attend the hearing and present their arguments in favor of or against the bill, as the case may be. As a rule it is in the committee that the fate of a bill is determined.

But once again it must be remembered that there is not in the states at each legislative session the laborious and painstaking discussion concerning the revenue that characterizes the meetings of the Committee on Ways and Means in the House of Commons. A scientifically equilibrated budget is unknown in our states. All that our state committees aim to do is to provide enough revenue. They do not consider each year a nice adjustment of rates in order that a certain and exact amount of revenue may be raised. Moreover, as has been indicated above, in a large proportion of the states the property tax is at the basis of the tax system and is also the elastic element in it, and the tax rate on property is in most cases either fixed by permanent statute or determined by some general rule that allows the rate to vary with the amount of the appropriations. This obviates, to a large degree, the necessity of regular tax acts which are usually considered as making up the revenue side of the budget.

(D) *Efficiency of the Committee System:*

The criticisms that are to be brought against the committee system from the point of view of the preparation of the budget are, in the main, two.

In the first place the committees cannot estimate accurately the needs. They meet in most cases only once in two years. Their personnel changes considerably from session to session. As a rule the members have had no administrative experience and they are therefore quite unable to judge of the validity of the arguments of the officers, etc. appearing before them. In view of these divers considerations it may be affirmed with confidence that the amounts that they decide upon are not likely to be as accurate as estimates carefully worked out by the responsible finance officers. That the committee's estimates are not accurate is proved by experience.

In the second place divided responsibility in budget matters renders a scientifically equilibrated budget practically impossible. This particular criticism is such a common one and so obvious that a mere statement of it is sufficient.

(E) *The Form of the Budget as reported by the Committee:*

(1) *The Scheme of Appropriations:*
Equilibrium and balance in the budget require that the full scheme of appropriations and the proposed plan for raising the necessary revenue be shown in juxtaposition before the budget is voted. There are, however, certain considerations which tend to lessen the importance of this rule and certain others which emphasize the tendency to disregard it when the attempt is made to apply it to the financial practices in the states.

In general it may be said that the scheme of appropriations, if carefully and sincerely drawn up, will embrace the expenditures that a wise policy makes necessary. Any material change in such a scheme would be therefore presumptively unwise, and so, as a rule, it is the revenue system which must be adapted to the scheme of appropriations rather than the reverse. This is the recognized practice and is responsible for the distinction between public and private finance that is usually expressed in the phrase, — more epigrammatic than accurate, — that "the state regulates its income by its expenditure while the individual regulates his expenditure by his income." But the revenue system is relatively a permanent one and the questions that usually come up relate only to the rates of taxation on certain permanent bases. A sound revenue system has certain elastic elements that permit a ready adaptation to changed requirements, but when the limits of the elasticity of such a system are reached it becomes obviously necessary to make changes in the system itself. This is another way of saying that new taxes are added to the revenue system only when expenditures begin regularly to outrun the income which at its maximum efficiency the system will yield. Consequently it is only when additional sources of revenue must be resorted to or when certain reforms in the system are planned that that part of the budget relating to revenue has to be very scrupulously studied by the legislature. The part relating to appropriations is thus normally the one that engages most attention.

It has been said before that in the American states the property tax is, as a rule, the backbone of the revenue system. In half of the states also the rate of the tax on property is either specified by general law or is determined according to general principles that are so specified. Where the state depends on other sources of revenue, as in New York, the rates of taxation are not subject to readjustment at each legislative session but are relatively fixed. In only a minority of the states, therefore, is the question of the revenue side of the budget one that has to be regularly considered. But even in such a minority of the states—dependent as they are upon the general property tax for the major portion of their revenue—it is a relatively simple thing for a legislative committee to determine what the necessary rate must be. The value of property increases slowly rather than decreases and is not on the whole subject to serious fluctuations and so the state is assured of most of its income irrespective of possible developments in the commercial world. This stability and certainty of the property tax renders the consideration of the revenue side of the budget in the states of little practical importance and therefore the rule that requires the presentation of the revenue plan as well as the scheme of appropriations in the projected budget, applies with only diminished force.

As a matter of fact it is not found anywhere in the states that the rule is observed. In only a few of the states does one committee have charge of both appropriations and revenue and only in such states would it be possible to have a comprehensive budget presented. Where one or more committees report appropriations and an entirely different committee has charge of revenue no single all-comprehensive measure is possible. But even in those states where one committee does have the oversight of both appropriations and revenue it is not the practice to report a single measure embracing a complete budget.[1] In most cases the committees could not report such a measure if they desired to do so. They report by bill and in a majority of the states there is some constitutional provision which would prevent the combining of appropriation and revenue measures in one bill.[2] In these cases the constitutions themselves preclude the possibility of the application of the rule. In view then of the practice of the various states, as enforced by constitutional provision or long custom, it becomes necessary to consider the two parts of the budget independently. Attention will therefore be directed first to the appropriation measures and secondly to the revenue measures.

(2) *Appropriation Measures:*

(A) *Constitutional Restrictions:* In almost half of the states of the Union there are constitutional restrictions which militate against the presentation of a complete and well balanced scheme of appropriations. Twelve states have restrictions definitely limiting the scope of the general appropriation bill. Six of these[3] have provisions that are almost exactly similar. In these states the general appropriation bill is limited to ordinary expenses of the executive, legislative and judicial departments of the government, interest on the public debt and for public schools.

[1] The South Carolina legislature passes at each session an act entitled "An Act to raise supplies and make appropriations for the fiscal years," etc., but as a matter of fact this is only a revenue bill. There is a separate bill for appropriations.

[2] See preceding chapter — "Restrictions concerning legislative procedure."

[3] Alabama, Colorado, Mississippi, Montana, North Dakota, and Wyoming.

The Arkansas constitution excludes even the appropriations for school purposes and for public debt. In Georgia there is a wise provision which enables such appropriations as are fixed by previous laws to be included in the general bill, the provisions regulating which are otherwise like those in the six states mentioned above. The provisions of the South Dakota constitution are also similar to those of the six states referred to above except that they permit the general bill to include also the appropriations for the state institutions. In California the general bill is limited to the "expenses of the government," salaries of the state officers and appropriations for the state institutions. In Louisiana the bill may include only appropriations for the public schools, expenses of the government and interest on the public debt. Moreover in all of the states above referred to there is found the added provision that all other appropriations " shall be by separate bill each embracing but one subject."

In four states [1] bills making appropriations for salaries of the officers of the government and members of the legislature can contain no provisions on any other subject The Oregon constitution has a similar provision except that it allows "other current expenses of the government" to be included in such a bill.

The objects of restrictions of this kind have been already referred to in the preceding chapter. A bill for expenses of the state government is such a "strong bill"—(i. e., so sure of being passed)—that it becomes always a favorite agency for carrying through certain "riders," as they are facetiously called—which could not possibly go through the legislature on their own merits. These riders are tacked on sometimes by a combination of those who have special in-

---

[1] Florida, Illinois, Nebraska, and West Virginia.

terests to serve and who support one another's projects and sometimes by the majority leaders themselves as a sop to certain malcontents whose votes are needed for some important party measure. In this way the public money has often been foolishly expended. Very early this danger was appreciated and that is why so many of the states have so strictly limited the scope of the general appropriation bills.

In some states also the scope of the appropriation bills is limited by the rules of the legislature. Thus Michigan and Minnesota have a legislative "joint rule" which provides that bills making appropriations for state officers shall be limited to that purpose exclusively. Whether such restriction is imposed by the legislature upon itself or by the constitution of the state, the object is the same.

Consequently in the states where these restrictions—however imposed—obtain, a complete scheme of appropriations—always excluding of course those necessarily incidental—is possible only to the extent that such restrictions embrace all the activities of the state's government. Whether they do as a matter of fact depends very largely upon the interpretation put upon them. A broad interpretation would from the financial point of view be desirable.[1]

[1] It may occur to the reader that what has been said concerning the "form" of the budget ought in reality to come under the chapter on "voting." But it has been assumed all along that a complete scheme of the appropriations ought to be presented to the legislature first of all, irrespective of the various combinations that might be made for the mere purpose of voting. The trouble is that our legislative committees report only by bill, and although it is thoroughly sound to vote the appropriations in small groups, it is not sound to introduce such appropriations piecemeal, without in some way showing the relations of each to a whole scheme. A just balance between the parts cannot be obtained in this way. The committee may have worked out an entire scheme beforehand, but the legislature as a whole has a right to consider this also for itself. That this is not entirely unrecognized is shown by the provisions

There are however twenty-seven states where practically no restriction is placed upon this particular phase of financial practice and in these, at least, it would be possible, even without changing very much the practice of the committees reporting by bill, to have a comprehensive scheme of appropriations reported.

(B) *General Appropriation Bills:* All but eleven states [1] have what approximates a general appropriation bill. They vary considerably in scope and general content. It would be manifestly impracticable to describe the bills separately and therefore only general statements will be made. It may be said that in less than a dozen states do the general appropriation bills, as reported by the committee, embrace all the regular appropriations.[2] The appropriations not contained in the general bill are provided for in separate bills of which there are usually a considerable number. This militates against a proper balance in the appropriations. As a rule also, the general bills are not broad enough in scope and in almost all cases they are not carefully worked out and have to be supplemented with additional appropriations. A few examples will illustrate some of the shortcomings referred to. In Alabama in 1903 after the general appropriation bill was passed a number of other bills really incidental to or connected with matters in the

in Rule 27 of the Assembly of California which says "The Committee on Ways and Means shall from time to time, at least once in two weeks, report to the House the exact condition of legislation involving appropriations, and the aggregate amount of all the proposed appropriations pending."

[1] Connecticut, Illinois, Kansas, Kentucky, Massachusetts, Montana, Michigan, New Hampshire, North Carolina, North Dakota and Wisconsin.

[2] The following states have the most satisfactory general bills: Indiana, Maryland, Minnesota, South Carolina, Tennessee, Texas, Utah, Virginia and Washington.

general bill were introduced and passed and the general bill itself was amended later in the session. New York has three general appropriation bills,—all related to each other, — the "General Appropriation Bill," the "Annual Supply Bill" and the "Annual Supply Bill—Supplementary." In the first bill the theory is to include only the absolutely necessary expenses. The Supply Bill is supposed to make up the deficiencies of the previous year, increases that are allowed and such unforeseen expenditures as may have become necessary since the passage of the "general bill." The "Supply Bill—Supplementary" is supposed to gather up all the loose ends, so to speak,—in other words, to take care of anything that has been overlooked. It comes at the very end of the session. In 1905 the legislature of Maine had to pass a supplementary appropriation bill a little over a month after the first bill providing for the expenses of the government was passed.

(C) *Separate Large Bills:* In six states the appropriations are divided among a few large bills or among many smaller ones. In Illinois, Kansas and Montana the regular appropriations are divided among a few large bills although in Illinois there are more of these than in the other two states. In Massachusetts and Michigan there are a large number of separate bills. In Connecticut there are three different kinds of bills—"specific appropriations" which, as their name implies, are for the expenses of specified officers, etc.; "annual appropriations" which are practically permanent; and a bill for "sundry purposes" which provides the appropriations for all such expenditures as are authorized by the general statutes. In none of these states, then, is the requirement that the scheme of appropriations be presented as a well-balanced and comprehensive whole even approximately met.

(D) *Appropriations by General Statute:* Five states [1] have most appropriations provided for by general statutes. These states cannot be said to have any budget at all. Such appropriation measures as are reported are appropriations for special purposes or amendments to appropriations permanently provided for. From the point of view of budgetary balance no particular criticism can be urged against the practice of permanent appropriations. The practice in the long run may tend even to promote a just balance between the regular expenditures of the state.

(E) *Classification and Itemization:* Another question which seems to demand some consideration at this point is that of the classification and the itemization of the contents of the appropriation bills. Professor Adams points out [2] that there is a conflict in this particular between the administrative or the financial and the constitutional interests involved. His view is that although the constitutional interest demands particularization and itemization, the financial interest demands a few general classifications that allow the administrative department a wider discretion when once the measure becomes law. There is however some question whether administrative efficiency itself, in the states, might not be furthered by more complete itemization —especially in those states in which the governor is given the power to veto items in appropriation bills. This opinion is based on the consideration that financial responsibility in the states is a legislative rather than an administrative responsibility. Where the officer at the head of the finances of a state is responsible for the state's fiscal policy, as is the case with the Chancellor of the Exchequer in England, he watches closely how the money is spent and is in

[1] Kentucky, New Hampshire, North Dakota, North Carolina, and Wisconsin.

[2] *Science of Finance,* p. 143.

a position to rebuke a misuse of such discretion as may be allowed to any officer of the government in the expenditure of funds. But in our states where the responsibility rests upon a legislative committee, which meets,—in the great majority of cases,—once in two years and which has to get its work done within a prescribed number of days, the same careful oversight cannot be maintained. Under such circumstances a wide discretion in the expenditure of public funds might result in evils and abuses that could not be readily corrected. The abuse of "contingent funds" in both the national and the state governments would seem to be a case in point.[1] Furthermore in those states in which the governor may veto items in appropriation bills, it is apparent that the more detailed the appropriations are the more effectively can he exercise an oversight and control over his subordinates. Further reference will however be made to this in a later chapter.

As a matter of fact there can be found various kinds of classifications and all degrees of itemization. In general the classification follows the great divisions of government with the various subdivisions that come naturally under each; but in a few states, as in Maine for example, no attempt at classification is made.

In most of the states provision has to be made for two years and it is interesting to note in this connection what methods are employed in distinguishing the allotments for the two years. In some states [2] the amounts alloted for each purpose are shown in two columns, one column for

[1] The South Carolina constitution absolutely forbids appropriations for contingencies. So far as the national government is concerned, it happens that only recently (1906) there was a great outburst against contingent funds in Congress. The Department of State paid several thousands of dollars out of its contingent fund for a portrait of Senator Knox which was hung in the quarters of the Department of Justice.

[2] Mississippi, Colorado, Nebraska, and South Dakota for example.

the first year and one for the second. In other states[1] there are practically two bills, one for each fiscal year. In Florida the general appropriation bill is divided into four sections. The first section provides the appropriations for six months of the fiscal year that is current when the bill goes into effect, the second section makes the appropriations for a full year immediately following, while the third section makes the appropriations for the six months which follow such a year. Then in some states[2] the bill as reported simply names a certain amount which must suffice for the two years. In other states[3] the apportionments for the two years are shown in separate sections. In Minnesota the bill provides that the appropriations stated are available for each of the two fiscal years except in cases specified. In Virginia there are practically two complete bills—one for each fiscal year—although they are reported as sections of the same bill.

In the matter of itemization also the practice varies greatly. In New Hampshire where permanent appropriations are in vogue most departments are allowed to spend a certain amount per year—with no particular specification of purpose. Where permanent appropriations of this kind are the rule the provisions must of necessity be general. In South Carolina—at the other extreme—rigid itemization is practiced. In New York the tendency is toward further itemization—according to Mr. Jas. C. Rogers, for several years the Chairman of the Assembly Committee on Ways and Means—and avowedly with the purpose of giving the Governor a larger control over appropriations.

(F) *Regularity in Form:* Another point worthy of some

[1] Delaware, Maine and Maryland for example.
[2] Georgia and Missouri for example.
[3] Illinois, Montana and Indiana for example.

mention is regularity in the form of the appropriation bills. This may be passed over hastily. As a rule it may be said that the requirement of regularity in form is met more or less completely. From session to session there seems to be ordinarily little change although when longer periods are taken into account the change may be considerable. The changes are not however arbitrary and confusing but are as a rule the result of changed conditions which are in turn the result of new legislation.

(3) *Form of the Revenue Bills:*

Concerning the revenue side of the budget little need be said in addition to what has been said already. In half of the states (23) the revenue is provided according to general law which does not have to be re-enacted each year. In all such states the rate of the tax is fixed or a general rule of calculating the rate according to the authorized appropriations is laid down.

The other states do however regularly enact revenue measures which may be considered the revenue side of the budget and the point to be discussed is the form in which such measures are presented. In four states [1] the tax measure is brought in simply as a bill levying certain specified rates on property. The total rate alone is given in each case. In New York the only regular tax act is a similar measure levying the tax for the canal debt sinking fund.[2] In four other states [3] the tax bill is brought in as an amendment to the general statutes. In these cases also the rate is prescribed. In nine states [4] the practice is

[1] Alabama, Florida, Mississippi, and Montana.

[2] By constitutional amendment this charge is now met by the regular funds in the treasury. There is thus no longer in New York a direct tax on property for state purposes.

[3] California, Kentucky, Louisiana, and Maryland.

[4] Idaho, Illinois, Iowa, Kansas, Maine, Massachusetts, Minnesota, New Hampshire and Utah.

to report bills that express in dollars and cents the amounts that are to be levied, and some state officer or board afterwards calculates what the rate shall be. In two of the New England states [1] the bill specifies the amount that each town is to raise and it is left to the town authorities subsequently to determine the necessary rate. In New Hampshire the bill orders a lump sum levy and authorizes the treasurer to draw on the various towns according to the apportionment that is the standard at the time. The apportionment is changed from time to time. In Illinois instead of a lump sum levy, the practice is to report a measure which enumerates the several purposes for which taxes are to be levied and the amount required for each of such purposes is specified. In Georgia, however, practically the whole revenue system is re-enacted each year.

Three of the states have certain peculiar customs which deserve special mention. In Florida the bill as reported by the committee fixes a certain rate of taxation but it also contains a clause which authorizes the governor to reduce the rate if he finds that the aggregate assessment of either or both of the fiscal years of the biennium will permit it. Then the custom also prevails in Florida to report a special tax bill for pensions. In Michigan the custom is to include in most of the appropriation bills a provision which authorizes the auditor to include in the taxes to be levied a tax that will suffice to produce the amount so appropriated. That is to say, in most appropriation bills the ways and means for raising the money authorized to be expended are provided in the bills themselves. For the general and variable expenses of the state government however there is reported a special bill which levies a specified rate and which is known as the General Budget Bill. In South

[1] Maine and Massachusetts.

Carolina the bill as reported provides not only for the various state levies but also all the authorized county levies. The counties are enumerated in alphabetical order and under each county the rates for all the various purposes—state and county—are specified.

Throughout this chapter the attempt has been made to give a general view of the methods of preparing the budget in the states. It is hoped that the following points were made clear in Part I: that the executive and administrative officers have practically no control of financial matters but that the legislature alone is responsible; and that this is due largely to our form of government but also to the attitude of the legislature itself as well as to the comparative freedom from financial stress. In Part II the object was to show in a general way how the budget as a project of law is really prepared. This necessitated some account of the financial committees in the states because these committees are in reality the finance ministers. Then owing to the practice in vogue in the legislatures it became necessary to take up the two sides of the budget separately and to discuss its preparation from the point of view of appropriations and of revenue. The appropriation measures were considered most important because of certain general considerations and because of the tax system that obtains in most of the states. Some criticisms were ventured from time to time as the various questions were discussed. These criticisms may be summed up in the statement that no attempt is made to prepare a well balanced, equilibrated budget and that this gives rise to carelessness and wastefulness.

In the next chapter an attempt will be made to follow the budget in its career toward final legalization.

CHAPTER III

THE VOTING OF THE BUDGET

I. *THE ORGANIZATION OF THE LEGISLATURE:*

(*A*) *Comparison of American and Foreign Conditions:* Both M. Stourm and Professor Adams point out that in all constitutional governments the first step in the voting of the budget is the examination of the project by a commission or a committee of the legislature. As both authors show very clearly how this process is carried out abroad, it would be superfluous to give here any account of the foreign methods. We shall therefore proceed at once to indicate what seems to be the essential difference between them and the methods in vogue in the United States—and more particularly in the several states.

In parliamentary governments the budget goes through two stages. As reported by the finance minister it represents a scheme that has been carefully prepared by the "government." The government has itself considered the needs of the various administrative departments, etc. and in preparing its scheme has had in mind the maximum attainable efficiency of each department. In the first instance the scheme of estimates is thus based upon considerations of pure administrative efficiency. But in the second instance the government has had in mind also the possibilities of the financial system and has perhaps had to modify estimates based upon considerations of administrative efficiency in order to harmonize them with the possi-

84 [200

bilities of the financial system as such possibilities may be interpreted. Such then, is the first stage through which the budget goes,—the stage in which emphasis tends to be laid on administrative efficiency and fiscal expediency.

The second stage of the process is the examination by a separate legislative commission or committee. Such a commission ought to be,—and generally is,—one that represents a diversity of interests and political views. In England the ablest opposition leaders are always present at the meetings of the Committees of Supply and on Ways and Means; and in France, although the examining commission is chosen by lot, that very fact would tend to insure a representative from every important group in the Chamber. In the examination by this commission the point of view that becomes most prominent is a political one. Administrative efficiency and fiscal expediency are not and cannot be overlooked but they are interpreted in the light of political considerations by the various groups represented. In other words, in the second stage of the process, the emphasis is laid on political expediency.

In our states the budget as a report differs very materially from the budget in its initial stage as it is reported by the finance minister in England, for example. This was shown to be especially true of that part of the budget as a report which contained the estimates of receipts and expenditures for the ensuing fiscal period. In England the budget as reported by the Chancellor of the Exchequer is the actual basis of the budget that is ultimately voted by Parliament but in the United States the budget is made entirely anew by the committees. The revised budget, whether reported as a single measure by a single committee or as a series of separate measures by single or separate committees, resembles more nearly in form and legal character the budget of the English Chancellor of the Exchequer than does the budget as originally reported by the finance officer in our American states.

The first stage of the process through which it was stated that the budget goes in England is thus, for all practical purposes, wanting in our states. The legislative committee essays not only to correlate administrative efficiency and fiscal expediency with political expediency—which is its logical function—but it determines in the first instance what the demands of administrative efficiency and fiscal expediency may be and harmonizes these two in such way as it sees fit. As a matter of fact under this system the questions of administrative efficiency and financial expediency are forced to remain in the background while the political considerations are always those that are most prominent. In other words the first stage of the process through which the budget goes before it is actually legalized tends, in our states, to be sacrificed for the benefit of the second stage.

There is however a practice in some of the states which would seem to suggest an analogy to the English method. In about half of the states it is found that before a bill may be acted upon by the house it must be considered in a committee of the whole. In England, it will be remembered, the House resolves itself into a committee of the whole when studying the budget, the Committee on Supply when considering appropriations and the Committee on Ways and Means when studying the revenue side of the budget. Although in England these committees are technically committees of the whole, as a matter of fact only the leaders of the various parties and those especially qualified to take part in the discussion of fiscal matters attend the committee meetings. But in our American states where the practice of considering bills in committees of the whole obtains, there is not this fine sifting of the experts for the study of financial legislation. The rules of the house apply with slight modification to the committee of the whole. Debate is usually unlimited in the committee sessions, no stenographic record is kept and the ayes and noes cannot be called for. There is one point, however, which alone proves fatal to an attempt to establish the analogy referred to. The quorum for the committee session is the same as the quorum for the regular house sessions; this prevents any sifting of the abler men and attacks the analogy at its vital point. The ex-examination of the budget in the committees of the whole in the states is perhaps freer and amendments to it can be more easily secured than is the case when the house is organized in its usual capacity, but there is not that peculiarly careful examination which characterizes the English practice.

In the other states, where the rules do not require that measures be examined in committee of the whole, all bills are considered by the whole house under the regular rules.

(B) *Examination of the Budget:* The actual examination of the budget on the floor of the houses is not a long process. Appropriation and revenue bills are always given the right of way either by rule or by consent. This is necessary because the expenses of the state must in the first instance be provided for, while in the second place the funds with which to meet them have to be supplied. Since nothing is more important than this all other legislation must give way to it. In Pennsylvania for instance we find that Joint Rule No. 6 provides that when the general appropriation bill is reported in either house, it has priority over all other business until disposed of. Whether such preference is assured by rule or not, it is, as a matter of fact, everywhere accorded these measures.

A very general requirement in the states—found either in the constitutions of the states or in the rules of the legislatures—is that after a bill has been introduced it must be

88   THE BUDGET IN AMERICAN COMMONWEALTHS   [204

read three times. In some cases the reading must be on three different days although in others the first and the second reading may be on the same day. In almost every case however a sufficient majority may on the floor of either house suspend the rule. The first reading is for information only. The second is in most cases a reading of the title only. The third reading must be in full and is supposed to be important.

As a matter of fact very little attention is paid to the reading of the bills. The bills introduced are always printed and copies of them are placed in ample time on the desks of the legislators and therefore there is no need of listening to the clerk as with high-pitched voice and suspicious rapidity he performs the task of reading the bills. In some cases one can hear only the enacting clause followed by an outburst of unintelligible syllables when bang! goes the presiding officer's gavel and the clerk is ordered to proceed to the next bill or to the roll-call as the case may be. There is a rush and a go about the procedure in the legislatures that quite takes away the breath of the uninitiated onlooker.[1]

[1] As an illustration of the speed with which appropriation measures are sent through the legislature there is given here an account of the passage of the Miscellaneous Appropriation Bill in Kansas in 1901. It was introduced March 1st by the Chairman of the Committee on Ways and Means, after he had asked for the unanimous consent of the house. On motion of the chairman of the committee the rules were suspended and the bill was placed immediately on second reading. The bill was then read a second time. Immediately the committee chairman asked unanimous consent to have the rules again suspended, to have an emergency declared and that the bill be *considered* engrossed and placed on the Calendar under the heading of "Third Reading of Bills" subject to amendment and debate and that a sufficient number of copies of the bill be printed for the use of the Senate and House the same day. On the next day, March 2nd, the bill came up for third reading. The bill was amended somewhat but was carried and then went to the Senate. On the same day the chair-

Amendments:

Whether the financial measures can be amended or not depends at any one time upon the strength of the majority and the stage to which the committee system has developed. Where the majority is strong and the power of the committees is great it is practically impossible, when party discipline is maintained, to make an amendment that is unsatisfactory to the party leaders of the majority. Party discipline is not so rigid in the states as it is in Congress and the committee system is not so fully developed [1] so that

---

man of the Senate committee moved that the rules be suspended and that the bill be read the first time. The motion prevailed. After the reading the chairman moved that the rules be again suspended, an emergency declared and the bill be read a second time. This motion also prevailed. The bill was read and referred to the Ways and Means committee. Later in the day the chairman asked for unanimous consent to report the bill. Consent was given and the bill was reported favorably but with a number of amendments. The report of the committee was adopted, the bill was read a third time and passed. Still on the same day the bill as amended was reported back to the house and the chairman of the House Committee on Ways and Means moved that the House non-concur in the Senate amendments and that a conference committee be appointed. The motion prevailed and three conferees were appointed on the part of the House. On the same day the Senate appointed two conferees. That same day the conference committee reported to the House and to the Senate and the report was adopted without amendment. In other words it took only two days to introduce an important appropriation bill, to have it amended on the floor of the House and then passed; to have it sent to the Senate, referred to a committee, reported by the committee with amendments and passed; to have it sent back to the House and then to a conference committee; to have it reported by the conference committee to both houses and finally to have the report of the committee adopted by each house before adjournment. How much examination of such a measure could have been given on the floor of either house?

[1] In New York where party discipline is certainly as strong as it is in any other state and where the committee system is developed more highly than in any other state the legislative session of 1906 affords two illustrations of this general assertion. The Tully-Wain-

on the whole it may be said that amending the finance bills is not such a difficult process in the states as it is in Congress.

The technical right to offer amendments is of course always provided in some form or other. When the bills are considered in committee of the whole amendments may be freely offered. If the amendments are adopted by the committee the fact is reported by the chairman when the committee rises to report to the house. Usually also the bills so reported are again subject to amendment on the floor of the house after the committee rises although there are some exceptions. In California for instance Assembly Rule 10 provides that appropriations can be increased only in committee of the whole. Where the bills are not considered in the committee of the whole the rules prescribe how amendments are to be submitted. The differences in the practice from state to state in this particular are immaterial. Suffice it to say that the privilege of offering amendments is everywhere guaranteed to each individual legislator although other considerations that are not technical in character determine whether the amendment can in reality be offered and whether it will ultimately be accepted or rejected.

In actual practice there is considerable variation from state to state. In the states where the measures are considered in the committee of the whole the journals disclose the fact that amendments, to appropriation bills at least, are freely adopted. That amendments are made in the committee of the whole that are sometimes repugnant to the committee which originally drew up the bill is shown, for

wright Local Option bill was taken out of the hands of the Assembly committee which had it in charge and which refused to report it and the repeal of the Mortgage Tax went through both houses despite the strenuous opposition of the majority leaders.

instance, by the amendment of the General Appropriation Bill in Indiana in 1903. The committee of the whole had made several amendments to the bill as reported by the Committee on Ways and Means; and when the committee of the whole arose to report, the Ways and Means chairman attempted to have three of the amendments stricken out. In only one case however was he successful, the other two amendments being allowed to stand. In the states where there is no examination of the bills by a committee of the whole the process of amendment is naturally more difficult. The approval of the committee reporting the bill is not always necessary before an amendment can really be made, although the whole tendency is toward strengthening the committees' power. Factional differences within the majority are the most fruitful causes of the downfall of the committees' power. Thus in the New York Senate some years ago a faction of the republicans united with the democrats to cut down the appropriation for the Superintendent of Elections in the metropolitan district.[1] As a rule however few amendments to appropriation bills—and none to the regular revenue or tax bill—are made by individual members on the floor of either house because the committees in their hearings give every interest a chance to be heard. The pros and contras are more or less carefully considered in committee and the general bills are passed in practically the same form that they are reported.

The Vote:

The actual roll-call is on the bill in its entirety. When all the regular appropriations are provided in one large general bill the mere act of registering the vote is thus not

[1] The democrats always maintain that the office was created to weaken them in New York City.

one that consumes much time. The practice does, however, prevent the legislature from voting on any particular part of the state's policy. On the other hand, where the regular appropriations are voted in a number of separate bills this particular inconvenience may be overcome but the element of balance is correspondingly jeopardized. In Ohio five senators and ten representatives may demand a vote on any item in an appropriation bill. This would seem to be a fair and logical compromise. Essentially, each item of an appropriation bill constitutes a separate enactment and the legislature ought to have a right to single out any particular item if it so chooses. It might be argued that this could be done by amendment in the regular way, but as a matter of fact a strong "house machine" might easily prevent an amendment for which a majority in the house would vote if an opportunity for voting were afforded. The Ohio rule permits the concentration of the legislature's attention on any part of an appropriation bill and helps to prevent the tacking-on of the baneful " riders." When the roll is called the legislators respond " aye " or " no " but in voting on the general appropriation bills the ayes always have it.

(C) *The Bill in the Senate:*

We assume here that the bill has originated in the lower house. As a matter of fact in more than a half-dozen of the states the regular appropriation bills originate in the senate.[1] This has however, so little significance from any point of view that no attempt will be made to distinguish between the states where the place of origin is the lower house and those where it is the senate. The procedure is practically the same in both houses. The bill then, after

[1] This matter was discussed in Chapter I.

leaving the house goes to the senate. Here it is immediately referred to the senate committee on appropriations—or whatever be its particular name in any state—and the whole process of examination is gone through with again. The senate committee receives communications, appoints hearings and conducts investigations. Of course it always finds something to amend and never hesitates to make an amendment wherever it seems advisable. Sometimes indeed it strikes out all of the house bill except the enacting clause and substitutes a new bill of its own. This is quite the fashion in New York. In only a few of the states are the amendments made by the senate in one general direction.[1] The various services provided for are studied according to their own merits and therefore, as a rule, amendments are made in the senate committees which increase some appropriations and cut down others. When finally in shape the bill is reported to the senate and the procedure is thenceforward practically the same as has already been described for the house.

The bill, when passed by the senate, has to go back once more to the house in order that the house may express itself as to the amendments that the senate has made. In a great majority of cases—although not with absolute regularity,—the house's decision is adverse,—that is to say it votes not to concur in the senate amendments and the bill must go to a conference committee.

(D) *Conference Committee:* The house and the senate are both represented on the conference committee. A few of the leaders of the house and senate committees on appro-

[1] The senate in California usually decreases the house appropriations—according to the Comptroller. The same is true of Delaware, Florida, Idaho and Rhode Island. The opposite is true in Indiana, Missouri, Maine and South Carolina.

priations — or whatever other name the committees may bear—are designated by the presiding officer of each house respectively. The committee then meets and endeavors to mark out a compromise measure. The conference-committee meetings are always rather strenuous because each side tries to hold out for its own contentions; but in the end, by mutual concessions, agreement is finally reached. The bill is then reported either to both houses at the same time or to one or the other as the case may be. The bill so reported almost always becomes the law, for amendments to the conference committee's report are everywhere frowned upon.[1]

It has been seen that the senates in the American states, unlike the House of Lords in England, take a very active part in budgetary legislation. The budget undergoes an examination that is rather different from that which is accorded the English budget. It is an examination which may tend to jeopardize "balance" in the budget but the second and independent examination on the part of the senate does usually insure one that is thorough.

The American process involves, however, a great waste of time and much futile labor, and there is little hope that such an uneconomical procedure can be modified. One original joint committee would be advisable if the

[1] Amendments to a conference-committee report are blocked in various ways. In the New York Assembly for instance the large appropriation bills after they have come from conference go to the Committee on Engrossed and Printed Bills and when reported printed by said committee, go to the Committee on Rules which always reports in favor of the passage of the bills *without amendment.* As the majority sees to it that this report is adopted amendments are then of course out of order. In the Senate also amendments are ruled out of order. Only in 1904 Senator Armstrong endeavored to have an item relating to assessments in the city of Rochester stricken from the conference committee's report on the Supply Bill but an objection on a point of order was sustained by the President.

committee's power over amendments were increased. In Connecticut the reports of the Committee on Appropriations — which is a joint committee — are simply "explained" on the floor of each house by the Chairman on the part of the House and the Chairman on the part of the Senate respectively and the reports of the committee are always adopted. In Minnesota, on the other hand, where also a joint committee originally reports the appropriation bills to House and Senate simultaneously, amendments are always made and a conference committee is necessary before unanimity of action can be obtained. The practice in Connecticut would seem to be, therefore, the one to be emulated.

After the bill has passed both houses its career in the legislature has been run. It is then proclaimed as a law or — in the states where the governor is given the veto power—is sent to the governor for his approval.

II. THE POWER OF THE GOVERNOR:

In all but four states [1] the governor enjoys the veto power. In twelve out of the remaining forty-one states the governor has simply a general veto power—but in the remaining twenty-nine he enjoys in addition the power to veto items in appropriation bills. But the veto power so granted is not absolute. In most of the states two-thirds of the members elected to both houses may overrule the governor's veto, while in five of the states a simple majority suffices to do so.[2] In Maryland a three-fifths majority is necessary, while in Wisconsin two-thirds of those present is all that is required. Moreover the governor must return the bill with his objections within a prescribed time, or else it becomes a law irrespective of what he may wish.

[1] Connecticut, Delaware, North Carolina, and Rhode Island.
[2] Alabama, Indiana, Kentucky, New Jersey, and West Virginia.

A few of the states allow the governor only three days to make up his mind;[1] a larger number allow five days; Maryland makes it six days, Pennsylvania, Ohio and a few others make it ten days while California allows twelve days. The practice is thus decidedly not uniform.

The general veto power is not very effective in budgetary legislation. The expenses of the state have to be provided for and it is inconceivable that the governor should object to an entire bill making provision for such a purpose. It is, however, very probable that certain items may seem objectionable to the governor or that certain items may be dispensed with in the interest of fiscal expediency. The power to veto items in appropriation bills is therefore the logical outgrowth of the veto power in general. Each item of appropriation is in essence a separate enactment and if the veto power be given at all it should be given in such a way that the governor may veto or approve each of such items.

Where the power to veto items in appropriation bills is given to the governor, it is found that he uses it very freely. In Ohio, where Governor Herrick was the first governor to enjoy the veto power, he as governor used his power so freely that he caused no end of resentment among the politicians. Moreover, the governor's veto on items in appropriation bills is rarely overruled. He usually has the best of reasons for exercising his veto and the fact is generally recognized. In addition to this the appropriations come as a rule near the end of the legislative sessions and it is therefore difficult to get another vote on vetoed items.

By his veto power the governor can make his influence felt in the adjustment of the appropriation side of the bud-

[1] Wyoming and Minnesota for example.

get—the side which is of course the most important. If the governor's administrative responsibilities were increased and if the various officers of the government had to submit to him their estimates and furthermore if the appropriation bills were more minutely itemized, he could, by means of his veto power, control to a large extent the state's policy of expenditure. This would seem to be an end worthy of achievement.

III. *THE BUDGET DELAYED:*

M. Stourm, in his chapter "Refus du Budget,"[1] has the following to say: "To refuse the budget! One can scarcely conceive of the consequences of such an eventuality. If the year were to open without the budget having been voted, the bondholders could not touch their interest nor the pensioners their pensions; the tradesmen would beat in vain at the gates of the Treasury; the officials would work and would receive no pay; the schools would be closed; the army would be deprived of its pay, of its livelihood even, of its equipment, of its provisions. All the tributaries of the state, that is to say practically everybody would find himself affected; the life of the country would be stopped." The picture that this quotation conjures up makes us stand in fear and trembling before the prospect of the failure to vote the budget in due season. Yet a large number of our states exhibit a most refreshing carelessness in this particular.

It must be said, however, that the consequences of the failure to vote the budget suggested here by M. Stourm, would not be nearly so appalling or so far-reaching in our states. He had his own France in mind where the national government does exercise an oversight over all the local organizations and where a refusal of the budget would

[1] *Le Budget*, p. 380.

in reality affect practically everybody. But in our country where national, state, municipal and even county governments are relatively independent the failure on the part of the state government to pass the budget on time would not have the direful consequences either extensively or intensively that would characterize a similar eventuality in France.

As a matter of fact in a large number of our states the budget is not passed until after the opening of the fiscal period for which it is intended. In nine states [1] the legislature meets in January shortly after the opening of the fiscal year itself, which in such states occurs on or about the first of the calendar year. In eight other states [2] although the legislature meets also early in January, the fiscal year—as was shown in the preceding chapter—begins one, two or three months before the opening of the legislative session. In these seventeen states then, unless some special arrangement is employed, there is bound to be a period when no appropriations for the expenses of the state are available.

There are however such special arrangements in some of these states. It was shown in the preceding chapter that Nebraska, Ohio and Tennessee have appropriation years that differ from, and are independent of, the respective fiscal years and thus appropriations are available for a period beyond the fiscal year. In Alabama, Colorado, Massachusetts, West Virginia and Rhode Island other provisions are made. In Alabama the general appropriation bill which makes appropriations for a period of four years,

[1] Delaware, Idaho, Maine, Missouri, Nevada, Rhode Island, South Carolina, Utah, and Oregon.

[2] Alabama, Colorado, Massachusetts, Montana, Nebraska, Ohio, Tennessee, and West Virginia.

contains a clause that renews the appropriations made for the last year of such period, for the fiscal year immediately following up to February first. This constitutes a six months extension of the appropriation made for the last year of the period. In Colorado the legislature soon after the opening of its session makes haste to pass what is known as the " Short General Appropriation Bill " which makes provision for the first four months of the fiscal year current. In Massachusetts the general statutes [1] provide that the officers or boards may continue their several departments for a period that approximates two months, after the close of the fiscal year, at the rate of expenditure authorized by the appropriations during the preceding year. In West Virginia the General Appropriation Bill contains a provision which authorizes the auditor to make payment, to enumerated officers and institutions, during the first six months of the fiscal year immediately following the second year of the biennium for which the general bill provides, of sums of money not exceeding in the aggregate one-half of the amount appropriated for the officers and institutions specified for such second year. In Rhode Island the General Treasurer is authorized to pay one-sixth of the annual appropriations. Nevertheless, in Alabama, Colorado, Ohio and Tennessee, despite these special provisions, appropriations for the expenses of the state are regularly or occasionally late, that is to say, there is a period when no money for the expenses of the state is available. In the other states where the legislature does not convene until after the opening of the fiscal year and where there is no special arrangement for bridging over the intervening period an hiatus of this kind is bound regularly to occur.

Moreover, even in some of the states where the legis-

[1] *General Laws of Massachusetts*, Chapter VI, Sec. 40.

lature does meet before the opening of the fiscal year, it not infrequently happens that the appropriations of one period lapse before those for the ensuing period are legalized. This has been true recently in Arkansas, Nebraska and Virginia.

The question naturally arises, what is done in these periods when no money is provided? Do the activities of the state cease? We all know of course that they do not. As a rule, those who have claims for services rendered or materials furnished during such a period, trust the legislature to make good such claims, and it goes without saying that the legislature always recognizes this obligation. The officials do not quit their posts and the state never experiences any difficulty in obtaining the supplies it needs. Officials and claimants simply wait for their payment until the necessary appropriation is made. Sometimes extra-legal expedients are tried. In Delaware for instance, " the state treasurer assumes the risk and keeps things moving." In Nevada "the banks advance the necessary money."[1] The fact remains, however, that in a considerable number of our states there are periods when officials have to go without their pay, when the state institutions have to be run on "trust" and when private individuals have to make advances of money or materials in order that the activities of the state may not be brought to a halt.

This is an undignified and humiliating situation for which the fact that no great harm results is but a slight palliation. It is a petty thing for a great state to make its servants wait for the compensation that is justly theirs and it is undignified to expect private individuals to step into the breach and to provide the funds whereby the activities of the state may be continued. Some special provision ought

[1] These quotations are taken from correspondence of the state officials.

to be made or the fiscal year ought to be changed to conform to the practice of the legislature in legalizing the appropriations, in order that a condition of this kind could not arise.

IV. THE APPROPRIATION PERIOD:

(A) *Lack of Importance:* The question whether all the public moneys should be voted at each regular session of the legislature or not is one that involves, for the most part, purely constitutional considerations. The question as usually put is, whether all moneys should be voted annually or not, but in our states—owing to the fact that in a great majority of them the legislatures meet only biennially—the question would have to refer to a biennial rather than an annual period. But since the question is one whose great significance rests upon considerations of constitutional law it is not one that, from the point of view of finance, has, in our states, very much importance.

The practice of voting public moneys for only a year at a time arose because the people feared to make the executive independent of the legislature for any considerable period. It was considered dangerous to allow the executive any such independence. Money voted for a long period of time might easily be used for executive aggrandizement and for the defeat of the popular will. It was pointed out in the first chapter, however, that in our states there is no longer any fear of the executive, and that the problem in the states is one of administrative efficiency rather than of the establishment of constitutional principles. It would, therefore, serve no very useful purpose to linger for any great length of time upon this particular phase of the states' financial practice and little more than a cursory examination of it will be attempted.

(*B*) *Constitutional Provisions and Practice:* Some twelve of the states have constitutional provisions bearing on the question under consideration. In eleven states [1] these provisions specifically or implicitly limit all appropriations to two years, although it is suspected that they are aimed at the legislature rather than at the executive in such states. In Tennessee the courts have held that one general assembly cannot make an appropriation beyond the term of its existence.[2] Alabama also has the unique provision that no appropriation for a standing army can be made for a longer term than one year. In all the other states, however, the matter rests entirely in the hands of the legislature.

Turning, then, to the actual practice, it is found that a comparison of the various kinds of appropriations employed in the states with those employed by the general government will help to place the matter in a somewhat clearer light. In the practice of the general government there are three kinds of appropriations: (1) annual, (2) permanent annual, and (3) permanent specific. These are fully described by Professor Adams in his "Science of Finance."[3] The "annual appropriations" are those which have to be regularly voted by Congress each year. The "permanent annual appropriations" are for certain regularly recurring expenses which cannot possibly become the subject of political controversy, and which are therefore voted once for all. A certain amount of money stands annually appropriated for such various expenses until the law is changed or repealed. The "permanent specific ap-

[1] Arkansas, Illinois, Kansas, Louisiana, Mississippi, Missouri, Montana, New York, Ohio, Texas and Washington.
[2] Art. II, Sec. 24, Constitution—See *Annotated Code of Tennessee,* Nashville, 1896.
[3] Page 158.

propriations" are made for specific objects, and such appropriations stand until the respective objects so provided for are accomplished.

The appropriations in the states are similar in general nature, although the names applied to the various classes differ somewhat. The appropriations in the states corresponding to the federal "annual appropriations" bear, as far as could be discovered, no regular name. These appropriations will, therefore, in this place be considered under the name of "ordinary appropriations," because they have to do, for the most part, with the ordinary expenses of the state government. The state appropriations analogous to the federal "permanent annual appropriations" are most widely known as simply "annual appropriations." The "permanent specific appropriations" find their counterpart in the state "special appropriations," and it is under the latter designation that they are considered here.

(C) *Ordinary Appropriations:*

These are, of course, the most common. They cover the ordinary expenses of the state government, state institutions, etc., and are voted anew at each legislative session. They are included in the general or regular appropriation bills which are passed in most of the states. The appropriations expire ordinarily at the end of the fiscal period for which they are provided, and whatever balance remains reverts to some general fund of the treasury. There are, however, some exceptions to this general statement. In Maryland each appropriation is considered a separate and continuous fund and balances are carried forward from year to year. In Massachusetts, where there are annual legislative sessions, the appropriations run one year in addition to the years for which they were made. Practically the same is true in New York and South Carolina. In

Minnesota the state auditor " has the authority to extend all appropriations made in case of absolute necessity for the best interests of the state." In West Virginia appropriations may run three years, although the auditor writes that most of them are drawn before the expiration of the fiscal period.

(D) *Annual Appropriations:*

These are fixed by general laws, which remain on the statute books until changed or repealed by the legislature. They make a specified appropriation for a particular purpose for each year, and until the law is changed or repealed the amount specified is available for such purpose each and every year. In the case of these appropriations any unexpended balance at the end of each year is covered back into the treasury. "Annual appropriations" are very common in the states, almost every state in the Union having them in some form or other. They are, of course, more common in some states than in others. In North Carolina, New Hampshire, Kentucky, North Dakota, Michigan and Wisconsin almost the bulk of the regular expenditures are provided for by means of " annual appropriations." In a very large number of states the incomes of the permanent school and other trust funds and certain other moneys which may be regularly added to such sums are paid out each year without appropriation by the legislature. In most cases such appropriations are made according to constitutional requirements. School moneys, for instance, are simply apportioned each year according to some accepted basis of apportionment—usually the number of children of school age in each county.

As a sort of sub-class under " annual appropriations " must be mentioned those annual appropriations which are limited to a specified period of years. These make appropriations of particular amounts each year, for specified purposes, but only for two, three or four years, as the case may be. These appropriations thus lapse at the end of the specified period without further action on the part of the legislature.

(E) *Special Appropriations:*

These are extremely common and numerous. In a greater or less number they are made at each session of almost every state legislature. They are made for the accomplishment of a specified purpose, and until such purpose is accomplished the money is available. Where, however, constitutional provisions limit appropriations to any specific period, " special appropriations " are also of necessity governed by such provisions. If the purpose be accomplished before all of the available " special appropriation " is expended, the balance simply reverts to the general fund of the treasury.

On the side of revenue there is, of course, little to say. Revenue systems are necessarily permanent. The only question that arises here concerns the regular adjustment of the system to the needs of the state. It has been already shown how most of the states have general statutory provisions which make the regular voting of revenue measures unnecessary, and the other states where such measures are regularly voted were also referred to at sufficient length. Further consideration of the question at this point would, therefore, be superfluous.

After this rather hasty account of the periods of appropriation in the states the final point that remains to be considered in this chapter has to do with the discrepancies that arise between the estimated and the executed budgets and the means employed to overcome them.

V. THE DISCREPANCIES BETWEEN THE ESTIMATED AND THE EXECUTED BUDGET:[1]

Some discrepancy between the estimated and the executed budget inevitably arises. No human beings are endowed with prescience to such an extent that they can gauge with absolute accuracy the conditions of the future. Unforeseen exigencies are bound continually to arise. So in one particular or another the financial estimates that are originally made come wide of the mark. The discrepancy may be on the side of revenue or on the side of expenditure, and therefore some attention will be paid to each in turn.

(A) *Discrepancies between Estimated and Actual Revenue:* The discrepancy between estimated and actual revenue may involve a surplus or a deficit. A surplus is never the cause of much worry, and ordinarily there are no provisions concerning it. The revenue laws cannot be re-adjusted until the legislature meets, and the surplus must continue to grow until then. Florida has a unique statutory provision which allows the governor to reduce the tax rate on property if conditions seem to warrant it. The real problem in this connection, as Professor Adams points out, is to keep the surplus in the ordinary channels of trade. This has to do with the safekeeping of the public funds and will be taken up in a later chapter.

A deficit in the revenue yielded is, however, a more serious matter. When appropriations are authorized, the funds with which to meet them must be supplied. When the legislature has once adjourned and the rate of taxation has been determined, no way of increasing the tax levy presents itself. Other means of raising funds have, therefore, to be relied upon. The usual procedure is by some

[1] The author's debt to Professor Henry C. Adams is at this point obvious. At most other points in this dissertation it is just as great though perhaps not so obvious.

form of temporary loan to supply the needed funds until the legislature can provide additional sources of revenue.

A few examples of the means employed to this end will now be given, although it is not supposed that the question as to what particular form of temporary loan is used constitutes one of any great importance. A common practice is, when warrants are presented and no funds with which to pay them are at hand, for the treasurer to endorse the warrants "not paid for want of funds," after which the warrant draws a specified rate of interest—six or seven per cent. as the case may be in any particular state. Then when the treasurer obtains funds sufficient to liquidate some or all of the warrants so endorsed, he gives notice by mail or advertisement that the warrants outstanding and drawing interest will be paid. Within a period of time specified by law the payment of interest then ceases. Kansas and Iowa, for instance, allow a period of thirty days to elapse before interest ceases. In Idaho the prescribed period is ten days, while in California interest ceases immediately after the first publication of the treasurer's notice. As a rule, however, the rate of interest that a state would have to fix for unpaid warrants in order to guarantee the holders against any loss or depreciation would be higher than the rate of interest the state would have to pay if it were simply to borrow funds on its own credit in the market. Ordinary loans may, therefore, in the first instance be more economical. As a matter of fact these are generally provided for in the states, so that warrants may be paid when presented or quickly redeemed if out at interest.

A few examples of the means employed in this particular will, therefore, be useful. In Minnesota [1] the governor, auditor and treasurer are authorized whenever in

[1] *Laws of Minnesota*, sec. 519.

their judgment it becomes necessary, in order to meet the current demands of the revenue fund (which is the fund out of which the regular expenses of the state government are paid) to make agreements " with banks or other corporations or persons " to pay warrants issued against the revenue fund. For this service the designated officials may agree on the part of the state, to pay interest at a rate not exceeding 6% per annum until the state treasury can redeem the warrants so paid. The aggregate amount, however, is limited to $100,000. Furthermore, the state treasurer is authorized [1] to borrow and use temporarily from funds having an available balance in the treasury an amount not exceeding $200,000 to supply any deficiency that may exist in the revenue fund. In New York [2] the comptroller is authorized to make temporary loans from time to time as the legal demands on the treasury make necessary at a rate of interest not exceeding 5% per annum. "Transfer certificates" are issued for such loans, the interest of which is payable semi-annually and the principal at such time within seven years when the comptroller thinks that the state treasury will be able to pay the same. In West Virginia [3] the governor may raise temporary loans running eighteen months at interest not exceeding 2 cents per $100 per day in such amounts as may be necessary to supply the wants. In North Dakota [4] the state treasurer, with the advice and consent of the governor, may borrow money to meet warrants when funds can be obtained at a rate of interest not exceeding 8%. The auditor is directed

---

[1] *Laws of Minnesota*, sec. 315.
[2] *Laws of New York*, 1902, sec. 1, amending chap. 10, sec. 14, of the Finance Law.
[3] *Laws of West Virginia*, chap. 14, sec. 26.
[4] *Laws of North Dakota*, sec. 1330.

to issue "funding warrants" in place of those so paid. The funding warrants are limited to $80,000 and may not anticipate the needs of the state for a period longer than sixty days. In Louisiana[1] the governor and treasurer are authorized to provide a loan only for deficiencies that would prevent the state from meeting the interest on its bonds. In Kentucky, according to the auditor, if a deficit occurs in one fund a sufficient amount to cover it is borrowed from another fund. These examples will probably suffice to show some of the means employed to overcome by means of short-time loans, casual deficiencies in the revenue.

The constitutions of at least thirty-two of the states have provisions which limit the amount of indebtedness for such casual deficiencies of revenue that the respective states may contract.[2] The constitutions of Arkansas and Florida practically prohibit any new debt, while that of Louisiana allows a debt to be contracted only when the funds for the payment of the interest on the existing debt are not at hand. In twenty states[3] the aggregate amount of indebtedness for casual deficiencies that the state may carry at any one time is limited to amounts varying from $50,000 in Michigan and Maryland to $1,000,000 in New York and Pennsylvania. In Colorado the aggregate limit is placed at ¾ of a mill on each dollar of the assessed valuation of property in the state, and when such assessed value reaches one hundred millions of dollars the debt for casual deficiencies may never exceed $100,000. Idaho and Wyoming place a similar maximum limit at 1½% of the as-

[1] *Laws of Louisiana*, sec. 3798.   [2] See Chapter I.

[3] Alabama, California, Colorado, Georgia, Idaho, Illinois, Iowa, Kentucky, Maryland, Michigan, Missouri, Nebraska, New York, North Dakota, Ohio, Pennsylvania, South Dakota, Texas, Utah and Washington.

sessed valuation of the property in the state. Colorado also limits the amount of such indebtedness that can be contracted in any one year to ¼ mill on each dollar of the assessed valuation. In Missouri the constitution allows such a debt to run only two years, while in seven other states [1] the respective state constitutions provide that a deficit of one year has to be made good by a sufficient tax the following year. In the states which have no constitutional limitations upon indebtedness the legislature exercises full discretion.

(*B*) *Discrepancies between Estimated and Actual Needs:* A discrepancy of this kind might also include a surplus as well as a deficiency. It is only deficiencies, however, that require remedial action, and they alone will be considered here. These may be provided for in three different ways: (1) a supplementary budget may be voted; (2) deficiency bills may be passed; (3) administrative appropriations may be made. Administrative grants may in turn be made in three different ways: (*a*) by an increase in the appropriation made originally by the legislature; (*b*) by the transfer of a surplus of one service to some other service; (*c*) by placing in the hands of the administration a limited fund to be used at its discretion.[2] An attempt will be made to consider these in turn and to ascertain to what extent each may be employed in our states.

First of all, however, it must be said, that in all the states the attempt is made to discourage the practice of allowing deficits to arise. Various legal provisions may be found whose object is such discouragement. In Massachusetts,[3]

[1] Minnesota, Nevada, Oregon, South Carolina, South Dakota, West Virginia and Wisconsin.
[2] *Cf.* Adams' *Science of Finance*, p. 181.
[3] *Laws of Massachusetts*, chap. 6, sec. 40.

for instance, the laws provide that no officer shall make purchases or incur liabilities in the name of the commonwealth for a larger amount than has been appropriated for the service or purpose for which such purchases have been made or liabilities incurred, and the commonwealth cannot be held responsible for any excess. In Kansas [1] every official empowered to direct the expenditure of money is expressly prohibited from making any contract or agreement for any purpose whereby the expenditure of any greater sum shall be contemplated than is expressly authorized by law. A violation of this section constitutes embezzlement of the amount in excess of that expressly authorized by law and involves a possible punishment of five years at hard labor in the state prison. In other of the states the appropriation bills themselves provide that appropriations shall not be exceeded. A few examples illustrating the general character of such provisions may not be amiss. In Missouri a deficiency created is made chargeable to the officer creating the same. In North Carolina, also, officers are held personally liable for deficiencies and the treasurer is forbidden to pay out more than the amount appropriated. In South Carolina a contract or agreement by any state officer, providing for an expenditure in excess of the levy for any particular purpose is made a misdemeanor. In Tennessee an officer creating a deficiency can be held personally liable, the comptroller is forbidden to draw his warrant for any excess, and the treasurer is ordered not to pay any warrant overdrawing an appropriation. California has a provision that is rather novel. The general appropriation bill provides that not more than one-twenty-fourth part of the amount appropriated for each department or institution shall be expended during any one

---

[1] *Laws of Kansas*, sec. 7329.

month without the consent of the State Board of Examiners and not more than one-half of such appropriations during the first fiscal year. In the last place it is found that two states — Illinois and Minnesota — have constitutional provisions which necessitate a two-thirds vote for any increase, by one legislature, in the aggregate appropriations for expenses of government made by the preceding legislature. All such provisions, however, are but safeguards and not absolute preventives. Deficits will inevitably arise in this department and in that—at one time or another.

This leads us again to the means employed in providing for such deficiencies.

(1) *Supplementary budgets* are not used anywhere in the states. In the majority of cases the legislative sessions are too short to permit them. In three states there seem to be what might at first glance be called supplementary budgets. In Colorado there is a " Short General Appropriation Bill " that runs for four months and is then superseded by the " General Appropriation Bill " for the full fiscal term. This second " General Appropriation Bill " might, therefore, seem to be a " supplementary budget." As a matter of fact, however, it is the real budget, while the " Short " bill is only a temporary expedient put into operation to supply funds while the large bill is being prepared. In the same way, in New York, the Supply Bill or the Supply Bill-Supplemental might be considered supplementary budgets, whereas in fact the Supply Bill and the Supply Bill-Supplemental are simply amendatory acts. They do not supersede the General Appropriation Bill but simply make certain additions to it. Finally, in Ohio, also, there is a bill making partial appropriations, followed by the regular bill, but there is no supersession of the first bill on the part of the second in the way that a real supplementary budget

supersedes the original budget. In no other state is there any bill that approximates a supplementary budget even to the extent that characterizes the examples referred to above.

(2) *Deficiency bills* are the common means of granting additional funds in our states. Eleven states[1] have regular, more or less comprehensive deficiency bills, specifically so-called and limited to the purpose of supplying deficiencies, or bills that also carry original as well as deficiency appropriations. Thus Ohio has two regular deficiency bills, one for " authorized deficiencies " and one for " unauthorized deficiencies." In Kansas appropriations for deficiencies are made in the Executive and Judicial Appropriation Bill, although there are in addition occasional deficiency bills for special purposes. In New York the "Annual Supply Bill" carries most of the deficiency appropriations, while in Pennsylvania the General Appropriation Bill performs a similar function. In all the other states there are occasional or incidental deficiency bills when the necessity for them arises.

(3) *Administrative Appropriations:*

In a country where the legislature is so predominant as is the case here it is not to be expected that administrative appropriations of any kind will enjoy a great vogue. Some attention will, however, be given to each of the three possible ways of making such appropriations.

a. *Extension of Original Grants:* So far as it has been possible to ascertain the facts, it is in only two states that the administration is given the right really to grant additional allowances. In Connecticut the Board of Control, consisting of the governor, treasurer, comptroller and attorney-

[1] Arkansas, Idaho, Kansas, Missouri, Nevada, New Jersey, New York, Ohio, Pennsylvania, Rhode Island, and Texas.

general, may increase an appropriation by unanimous consent only. In North Dakota the governor, auditor, and secretary of state form an emergency board which may in extreme cases make additional grants. Petition is made by the department or institution needing such additional grant, and the board signs an order to the state treasurer and the auditor ordering that an additional amount be given.

In eleven other states,[1] however, the administrative authorities are vested with the power to allow officials to create deficiencies, and this approximates the power to make an additional grant, although further legislative action is necessary before the funds are really supplied. In California the State Board of Examiners, consisting of the governor, secretary of state, attorney-general, and an elected secretary of the Board, may, by a certificate in writing duly signed by every member of the board, allow any department, etc., to create a deficiency, and the matter is brought up before the next legislature, which provides payment. In Colorado the governor and the attorney-general may approve the creation of a deficiency if the necessity of its creation is caused by a casualty happening after the regular appropriation has been made. The auditor gives a certificate of the amount and the matter is reported to the legislature for final action. A section of the General Appropriation Bill in Idaho regularly authorizes the State Board of Examiners to permit deficiencies to be created. The Board issues deficiency certificates for the amounts authorized, and these are then provided for in the regular deficiency bill. In Massachusetts the general laws provide that if expenditure is made in excess of appropria-

[1] California, Colorado, Idaho, Massachusetts, Minnesota, Nevada, North Carolina, Ohio, Oregon, Utah and Washington.

tions the officer in charge of the same must, on or before January 15th, report to the auditor the details of such expenditure and the reasons therefor, and the auditor must make a special report of the same to the General Court early in its next session. Ohio has an emergency board consisting of the governor, auditor, attorney-general, and the chairmen of the House and Senate Finance Committees, and this board may authorize deficiencies, which are taken care of subsequently in the "authorized deficiency bill." At least four of the members of the board must approve such deficiencies, which means that the legislature practically maintains a veto power over such administrative authorizations. Without describing in detail the arrangements made in the other states of the eleven referred to, it may be said that there is in each some official or board empowered to grant authority to create deficiencies, but final action must always be taken by the legislature before the actual funds are forthcoming.

b. *The transfer of amounts from one appropriation to another* by the administrative authorities is in the states more or less completely under the legislative ban. In North Dakota the Board of Examiners may, in extreme cases, make such a transfer of funds, but the rule is, practically everywhere in the states, that an appropriation made for any specific purpose, may not be used for any other purpose. Stringent statutory provisions are aimed to enforce this rule. Some examples chosen at random will illustrate the general character of these provisions. In Maine,[1] for instance, the laws provide that "money appropriated for the various branches of expenditure in the public service shall be applied solely to the object for which the appropriation is made." Similarly in New York it is provided [2] that

[1] *Laws of Maine*, chap. 2, sec. 20.
[2] *Finance Law of New York*, art. 1, sec. 36.

"money provided for a specific purpose shall not be used for any other purpose." In North Dakota the laws declare[1] that no money "appropriated for any specific purpose or fund" shall be "used for or transferred to any other purpose or fund." Finally, in Oregon[2] a provision to this effect is found: "When any moneys shall have been collected or received by any officer for any distinct and specified object, no portion of them shall be paid or applied to any other object or purpose without due authority, but shall be kept a separate fund for such specified object." The section further provides for a punishment of $500 fine and six months' jail for a violation of its provisions. It would thus seem that this particular method of making supplemental grants enjoys no favor in our states.

c. *Independent Funds:* Almost all of the American commonwealths provide their respective governors with the means of obtaining funds in cases of emergency. Strikes and other disorders may necessitate the employment of the state troops, and the funds necessary for such a purpose must be always available. But funds so obtained or so placed in the governor's hands for military purposes, rewards for the arrest of criminals, etc., may not be used to supply deficiencies in the ordinary civil departments of the state government. In Colorado a certain fund is given to a board known as the State Auditing Board, which is composed of the governor, attorney-general and auditor, and to this board the chief officers of the departments, etc., make estimates of supplies needed and the board acts thereon. This is not, however, a fund which the administration can use at its discretion, but is one which must be employed for specific purposes. Indeed, it has not been

[1] *Laws of North Dakota*, sec. 1203.
[2] *Laws of Oregon*, sec. 3150.

learned that any state of the Union puts in the hands of the administrative authorities any fund — outside of the usual small incidental funds—which such authorities may use at their discretion.

In general, therefore, it may be said that legislative deficiency bills are by far the most important means of allowing supplemental credits in our states. The complete supremacy of the legislative bodies in matters of financial legislation and policy is maintained even in this particular.

VI. SUGGESTIONS FOR THE IMPROVEMENT OF THE BUDGETARY PRACTICES OF THE STATES:

The attempt to make any suggestions relative to the improvement of the budgetary methods in our states encounters some serious difficulties. At present there are forty-five states in the Union, and in no two of them are conditions exactly similar. Governmental theories, traditions, institutions and practices vary much more in our country from section to section and from state to state than is ordinarily supposed. It might easily be the case, therefore, that a suggestion made for one state would prove hopelessly inapt when applied to another state. Consequently when forty-five states are under consideration it is obvious that it would be futile to attempt to do more than make certain general suggestions that might be regarded as more or less applicable to all of the states.

In giving these suggestions we cheerfully acknowledge our debt to Professor Henry C. Adams. He has considered at some length the defects of the national system, and he gives some valuable suggestions relative to its reform. The defects of the national system are, to a greater or less degree, also the defects of the systems in the states, and the suggestions offered for the reform of the one may be applied with some modification to the others. All that is necessary in this place is thus little more than to apply Professor Adams's suggestions to conditions in the states, modifying them as these conditions seem to demand.

The attempt was made in the first chapter to show that the practice in the states was characterized by an absence of executive influence in the preparation of the budget. The peculiar fitness of the executive branch of the government for this important task is universally recognized, and therefore it may safely be suggested that the aim in the states ought to be to increase the influence and the authority of the executive in this particular.

The question that immediately presents itself is, of course, how can this aim be achieved? In the national government Professor Adams advises that the authority of the Secretary of the Treasury be increased. In our states, however, there is no officer who corresponds very closely to the Secretary of the Treasury. The comptrollers and the auditors of the various states stand in somewhat the same relation to the state fiscal organization that the Secretary of the Treasury does to the national organization, but notwithstanding this there seem to be certain considerations which make it appear advisable to throw the responsibility of the administration of the fiscal system generally, and that of the preparation of the estimates in particular, upon the governor rather than upon the auditor or comptroller. In the first place, the ordinary state auditor has too many routine duties to enable him to exercise the complete oversight over general conditions in the state that the preparation of the budget would demand. In the second place— and this is really the important consideration—the administrative organization of the state is not so complex as it is in the national government. The governor has no formal cabinet, as is the case with the President, and the tendency in our states is to hold the governor personally responsible for the administration. As the comptrollers and auditors are, in the great majority of cases, officials elected by the people, the governor cannot be held responsible for officials who are thus thrust upon him. Furthermore, he is in a position to exercise a complete oversight over general conditions in the state, and the natural dignity and authority that his office already bears would make much easier the task of vesting him with the added financial authority in question than of vesting it in the auditor or the comptroller.

It is assumed, then, that it would be advisable to give the governor increased authority over estimates. The under-officers ought to submit their estimates to him. He would, of course, have always to consult the auditor or the comptroller and advise with him, but the chief responsibility should rest upon the governor himself. The two officials thus working together could prepare a budget by which the administration would be willing to stand.

Then, in the second place, the under-officers should not be allowed to appeal to the legislature over the governor's head. If such officers are dissatisfied with the governor's estimates for their departments they ought not to be allowed independently to appeal to the legislative committee considering the budget, but their complaints ought to come through the governor's hands. If, however, such suggestion be considered too radical, somewhat the same result could be obtained by giving the governor the veto power over items in appropriation bills and by providing at the same time that such bills be carefully itemized. The governor could thus veto the items that seemed to him objectionable. As a matter of fact, the governors of twenty-nine states already enjoy this power, and as state constitutions are amended with relative ease, the remaining sixteen states could without much difficulty vest their governors with a similar authority.

The budget as so presented by the executive could not, of course, have any legal value under our institutions. The right of the legislature to initiate all legislation is too fundamental even to suggest the possibility of modifying it in matters concerning the public moneys. If, however, all communications of the employees and officers of the state to the legislature had to be made through the governor as the superior executive officer—as would seem only fitting under any circumstances—and if, while the governor enjoyed the right of vetoing items in appropriation bills, all appropriations for the expenses of the state were carefully itemized, it would seem fairly apparent that the budget as presented by the governor would carry with it an authority immeasurably greater than do those budgets reported to the state legislatures at the present time.

The second suggestion has to do with the divided responsibility over budgetary matters in the legislature itself. There is great diversity in this particular from state to state, but, as was shown in the preceding chapter, conditions as a whole in the states are better than in the national Congress. A few of the states do centralize the control of both appropriations and revenue in one committee and a considerable number of others give single committees final oversight over appropriations and revenue respectively, but as far as can be discovered the tendency as a whole is not toward this centralization of financial authority. Such centralized control is, however, necessary before a well-balanced and equilibrated budget is possible, and it would seem advisable that the practice in the states be developed with such an end in view.

Several ways of attaining this result might be suggested. A joint revenue and appropriation committee affords obviously the best means. Professor Adams points out how such a committee might be assisted in its work by the other committees if it should prove that the labors of a single committee in charge of all money matters would be too arduous. The fact that it works in some of the states even under latter-day conditions, as in Connecticut, would seem to indicate that the plan could be applied—not without some difficulty perhaps—in all of the states. Some unity of action between the two great financial committees could be assured by having the chairman and—let us say—one other member of each of the two committees regularly appointed to the other committee. The chairman of the committee on appropriations is usually the majority leader, and on the appropriation committee the minority leader also is usually placed. These two could, therefore, with peculiar fitness be appointed to the revenue committee as well. Whatever plan be adopted the aim ought to be to centralize the legislative control over money matters.

This suggestion naturally implies considerable augmentation of the committee's power. Assuming that there is one committee, it ought to have final say as to all financial bills however introduced and as to all amendments offered to such measures. It will probably never be possible to take away from individual members of the state legislature their right to initiate money bills, and in our states it is not obvious that it would be wise so to do were it possible; but nevertheless the committee in charge of financial—or perhaps better—budgetary matters should have the final authority in deciding whether measures independently introduced or amendments should be considered by the house at large. With centralized responsibility it is not likely that the committee would report measures that might endanger the financial equilibrium or interfere with the orderly application of a financial policy which the committee had already outlined.

Finally, it would seem necessary to refer once more to the questions of the form of the budget and the fiscal year. These questions were, however, treated at sufficient length in the previous chapter and it is unnecessary to repeat at this point such suggestions as were there ventured.

CHAPTER IV

THE EXECUTION OF THE BUDGET

A STUDY of the execution of the budget in the various states, if carried out logically and completely, would involve a thorough account of the revenue systems in such states, as well as an exhaustive discussion of the methods of financial administration. Execution of the budget means a carrying-out of the budget law and as, strictly speaking, all the money which comes into the state treasury and all the money which is paid out by the state finds a place in the budget law, an account of the execution of that law would involve the burden of telling what the various kinds of income are, how they are collected, and how, when thus collected, the money is disbursed. Such a task, if fully accomplished, would require several large volumes, and it is reasonably obvious, therefore, that in an unpretentious treatise of this kind some very definite limits have to be recognized.

The subject-matter of the chapter divides itself naturally into three parts, concerning, respectively, how the money of the state is collected, how it is kept when collected, and how it is paid out to those to whom the law declares it to be due. The divisions will be considered in the order suggested.

PART I. COLLECTION

The revenues of the states—neglecting borrowed funds, or what Professor Adams would call "anticipatory revenues"

—may be roughly divided into four classes: (1) revenue derived from public property; (2) revenue derived from fees; (3) revenue derived from fines and penalties; (4) revenue derived from taxation. Most of the states have public lands which they sell or lease and from which they thus derive an income; or they have more or less extensive public works, such as levees or canals; or they own shares in banks or railroads or other enterprises which yield some return. Then all of the states have systems of fees, more or less extensive, according to which certain special services which the state performs are charged for and which, consequently, are also a source of revenue. And in the same way all the states get some return from the fines and penalties that are levied in penal cases. Now if the attempt were made in this place, in order to give a logically complete account of the execution of the budget, to tell how the various states manage their public lands and sundry other kinds of public property, or to explain the various systems of fees, for what services charged and how and by what officers collected, or, in the last place, to show how, in the state courts, the fines and penalties are collected, it would necessitate the piling-up of a mass of details which, the author must confess, he has not sufficiently accumulated and which are really not of sufficient importance to warrant their introduction into a chapter of this kind. The great bulk of the revenue of the states is derived from taxation, the other sources are only incidental sources and suffer correspondingly in importance. For these several reasons, therefore, no very special attention will be given to the collection of revenue from any source other than taxation.

It becomes necessary to point out again, however, that there are forty-five states in the Union and that each state has a tax system more or less peculiarly its own. Some states, like Texas and Oregon, still have the early form of the property tax, which is practically the sum total of the tax system, while other states, like New York and Pennsylvania, have various highly specialized kinds of taxes that are administered each according to its own principle. Thus, from section to section and from state to state, there are, in matters of taxation, diversities so numerous that it becomes impossible within the limits here observed to go into any detail concerning them. The aim will be, therefore, to consider only the more common and the more important taxes and to tell in as general a manner as possible how they are assessed and collected.

I. *THE GENERAL PROPERTY TAX:*

The first tax with which we are concerned is, of course, the general property tax. In all but a few of the more progressive states it is still the very backbone of the revenue system and although it is universally assailed by financial writers it bids fair to hold its own for a considerable period to come.

The study of the methods employed in collecting the general property tax involves, in the first instance, a study of the methods employed in assessing it. Assessment is itself made up of two processes, the " valuation " or the determination of the taxable amount of the " base " and the calculation of the amount of taxes due upon any particular aggregate of " units " of the base. In general outline our task is then, to give some account of the methods of assessing the property tax and also of the methods of collecting the tax after the assessment or the determination of the amounts due have been made. The tax on the property of individuals will first be taken up, then on that of corporations in general and finally on that of certain special kinds of corporations.

(1) *The Property Tax on Individuals:*

Valuation: Uniformity and equality in taxation demand that the general process of valuation be under the direction of the state government itself. If the minor jurisdictions were given the power to decide what forms were to be used, what means employed, etc. in this important process, conditions would be intolerably worse than they are now—though admittedly bad enough. The state governments themselves uniformly decide what particular methods, forms, etc. are to be employed in the valuation of taxable property. In some states these matters are taken care of in the laws but in most of them the officer at the head of the fiscal system of the state or some special officer or board is charged with the duty of prescribing the rules and regulations pertaining to the business of valuation.[1] The point is that the first step in the process of valuation is always under the direct supervision of the state.

The actual process of valuation must however be carried on in small areas. In the first place the time is limited and this fact requires that the process be carried on simultaneously within areas that are small enough to allow a completion of the task before the end of the period allotted for the purpose. In the second place conditions from place to place vary and justice demands that an authority acquainted with local conditions evaluate the property in each district. It is, therefore, the uniform practice in the states to turn over to the authorities of the minor jurisdictions or to local agents the task of discovering and listing the property to be assessed and valuing it in the first instance.

[1] In Maryland, for instance, we find that such authority is vested in the State Tax Commissioner, in the Secretary of State in New Jersey and Vermont, in the State Board of Equalization in Utah, and so on.

A large number of states make the minor civil divisions of the states the assessment districts. In a great many cases the county is the assessment district and the county assessor is the responsible assessing officer. The township system according to which there is an assessor for each township is in vogue in the states formed from the North West Territory and in a few others. In some of these, however,—Indiana and Illinois for example—there is a mixed system. Not all counties are under township organization and in those counties where this system of organization has not been adopted the assessment is made by the county assessor for the county as a whole. In other states—Georgia and Florida for instance—the counties are divided into assessment districts and an assessor is simply appointed for each. Then in the New England States each town is responsible for its own valuation, the town assessors—one or more — being chosen at the regular town meetings. Furthermore, cities are often given a certain autonomy in this matter.

In making the valuation a distinction is uniformly drawn between real estate and personal property. There is a wide variation in the legal definition of these two forms of property, from state to state, but that is of little consequence here. Attention is simply called to the fact that although personal property is as a rule valued every year, in some of the states the valuation of real estate takes place only once in a period of years. But in all of such cases changes in value caused by improvements, on the one hand, or destruction, on the other, are periodically taken into account whenever the assessment of personalty is made.

As a first step in his task, the assessor takes the blanks provided for him and proceeds to get one into the hands of every person liable for taxes. These blanks vary in form from state to state, but in most cases they include an elaborate classification of property in order that every kind of property may be listed. The assessor carries the blanks in person to the home or place of business of each person liable for the property tax, or sends it by mail. The person in legal control of property liable must fill out the blank and thus indicate,—supposedly accurately and fully—the various amounts and kinds of property for which he is liable. He must then take an oath, administered by the assessor, to the effect that he has listed all his property, etc. The assessor is however given broad powers of examination. He may examine under oath the person making the statement, may examine books, subpoena witnesses, etc., or may cite the person to appear in court for such examination. Furthermore the assessor may place his own valuation on the property listed and need not accept that given by the person who did the listing. The law usually declares that all property should be valued at " full cash value " or " market value " but the assessor may uniformly determine for himself what such amount should be.

The assessment blank has to be filled out and returned to the assessor within a prescribed time. In case a person refuses to fill out his blank the assessor lists the property as best he can. Sometimes also persons refuse to answer questions or to take oath to their lists. For these offenses divers punishments are provided—the valuation of the property may be doubled or redress may be denied if the assessor's valuation is unjust or a money fine may be inflicted or the guilty person may even be thrown into prison. Every effort is supposed to be made to get all property liable entered on the tax lists and when so listed to have it valued according to some just and common standard.

In a few states the work of the regular assessors is supplemented by what may be called certain " secret service " assessors. In Ohio, for instance, we find what is known as the "inquisitor system," in Iowa the "ferret system" and in Kentucky the system of revenue agents. Wherever a system of this kind is found the methods employed are about the same. It is the "inquisitor's" business to "ferret" out all property that is not properly listed and to see to it that such property is then entered on the lists. He is paid a high commission (20% or thereabouts) for all taxes that are collected on the property which he has caused to be entered on the lists and this, of course, acts as an incentive to diligence and watchfulness on his part. Most critics claim, however, that all these systems are, on the whole, a failure and represent them as the final desperate attempts to enforce that which is really not enforcible.

When all the lists are in, the most arduous part of the assessor's labor is completed. He has then to prepare the "abstracts," "assessment books," etc. In the assessment books or rolls the taxpayers of his district are given in alphabetical order and the amount of each kind of property for which each individual is liable is shown. The assessor himself must then append to the assessment books his affidavit that he has to the best of his ability honestly carried out his duties as prescribed by law. This means, of course, that he has not willfully neglected to enter any property liable and that he has not willfully undervalued any that was listed. The assessment books with the lists made out by the taxpayers are then deposited with the proper authorities—usually the town or county clerks or county auditors—and certified copies or abstracts of the books are sent to the responsible state authorities. This ends the main work of the assessor.

The assessment books are then open for public inspection for a specified period, or a record of the valuations is published in a newspaper or duly posted, or the taxpayers are notified by mail of the amount for which they have been assessed. Naturally many will feel aggrieved and will desire to have their assessments readjusted. Inequalities will also inevitably occur as between locality and locality. Something must be done to remedy these things, and thus we find, in all the states, certain provisions for the equalization of assessments.

Equalization: Equalization of assessments includes considerations affecting not only the taxpayers as individuals, but also the various localities in the state—each assessment district compared with every other assessment district. To meet these several considerations various agencies have been contrived in the states and our purpose here is to take a general view of them.

Considering first the equalization of assessments between individuals, it seems rather obvious that each assessment district or unit of area should have an equalization board or authority of its own. In general it may be said that the smaller the assessment area, the more just is the assessment likely to be in regard to the individual taxpayers of such area, and the more accurately can it be reviewed. This would seem to be especially true of real estate.

In the states it is found that as a rule, some local authority for each assessment district has the power of reviewing the assessments of the property of the individual taxpayers in such district. In the New England states some town board is vested with the reviewing authority. In Connecticut and New Hampshire for instance the "Selectmen" of each town constitute the reviewing authority. In Maine and Massachusetts the assessors in each town sit as a board to which aggrieved taxpayers may appeal. In New Jersey each local district has "Commissioners of Appeal" or some other local board. In the same way it is found that in some of the western states where a number of the counties have township organization, there is some township board vested with equalizing power. These boards are variously formed, viz.: the Supervisor of the Township and two electors in Michigan,[1] the Board of Supervisors in South Dakota[2] and Washington,[3] the assessor, clerk and supervisor in Illinois,[4] the township trustees in Iowa,[5] and so forth. In the states where the county forms the assessment district we naturally expect to see the power of equalization vested with some county authority. In most of the states the county board of supervisors or the board of county commissioners constitute the county boards of equalization, although in others such county boards are made up in other ways. In Arkansas for instance the county board of equalization is made up of three citizens appointed by the Governor; in Indiana it is made up of the county auditor, treasurer and assessor;[6] in Nebraska, of the county commissioners, clerk and assessor;[7] in Oregon, of the county judge, clerk and assessor,[8] in Tennessee,[9] of five freeholders appointed by the Quarterly Court. In Georgia[10] the grand jury and in Louisiana[11] the "police juries" cor-

[1] *Laws of Michigan*, sec. 3851.
[2] *Laws of South Dakota*, sec. 2098.
[3] *Laws of Washington*, sec. 660.
[4] *Laws of Illinois*, chap. 120, sec. 86.
[5] *Laws of Iowa*, sec. 1370.   [6] *Laws of Indiana*, sec. 6381.
[7] Cobbey's *Laws of Nebraska*, 1903, sec. 10519.
[8] *Laws of Oregon*, sec. 3079.
[9] *Supplement to the Laws of Tennessee*, 1904 (757-823), sec. 33.
[10] *Laws of Georgia*, sec. 935. In Georgia a dissatisfied taxpayer may have his assessment reviewed by a board of three arbitrators, one of whom is chosen by himself, one by the comptroller, and the two arbitrators then choose a third. *Supra cit.*, sec. 839.
[11] *Laws of Louisiana*, p. 796, sec. 22.

rect the returns in their respective districts. In most of the states therefore, whatever be the particular assessment district employed, each of such local areas or districts has some local authority for reviewing the assessments of individuals.

Where the equalizing authority is thus vested in some board, the usual procedure is to have the assessor appear before the board with the assessment roll to which his affidavit is attached,—at a prescribed or a regularly called meeting of the board. The roll is then carefully scrutinized by the Board and errors, etc. are corrected. The board may subpoena witnesses, examine books, etc. Assessments can be raised or lowered although, as a rule, reductions can be made only on the petition of an aggrieved taxpayer. In case of a change in any individual's assessment he is usually given sufficient notice of the change made and a notice of this kind must always be given if the change be in the direction of an increase in the assessment. The individual affected is then given an opportunity to be heard. Thus on the one hand the board may hear the petitions of aggrieved persons and lower their assessments and on the other hand it may increase the valuation of property that seems to have been undervalued in the lists.

Appeals from the decision of such boards are variously provided for. Where the board exercises jurisdiction in an area less than a county appeal may, as a rule, be taken to the county board of equalization, to some civil board specially vested with the power of hearing such appeals or to some county court. In most other cases where any appeal is allowed it is only to the courts. In Tennessee [1] and New Jersey [2] however appeal may be taken to the State Board of Equalization. Then in a few states—Michigan and

[1] *Laws of Tennessee, Supplement*, 1897-1903 (sec. 757-823), sec. 38.
[2] *Laws of New Jersey*, 1905, chap. 67.

Minnesota for example—the decision of the local board is final and the assessment roll approved by the local board must be "conclusively presumed by all courts to be correct."[1]

It is to be noted also that in some of the states regular equalization boards are not provided but other means of relief are afforded aggrieved taxpayers. In Rhode Island, for instance, an aggrieved taxpayer simply petitions the common pleas division of the supreme court in his county which court is given original jurisdiction.[2] In Virginia also appeal lies directly to the courts.[3] In West Virginia in case of a difference between the owner and the assessor as to personalty, each chooses a "discreet voter" and the two voters thus chosen act as an arbitration board. Their decision or that of an umpire chosen by them is final.[4] In Georgia also, although the grand jury has general power to correct the assessment roll, an aggrieved taxpayer may in the first instance have his grievance adjusted by a board of arbitration. The taxpayer chooses one arbitrator, the comptroller a second and the two arbitrators then jointly choose a third. The majority then fixes the assessment.[5]

Thus in one way or another, in every state of the Union, some means—more or less adequate—are provided whereby a taxpayer is supposed to be able to have his property so valued that his share of the public burden in proportion to his property is no greater than his neighbor's. It is notorious, however, that none of these schemes works out as it should.

[1] *Laws of Michigan*, sec. 3852 *et seq.* Of course for constitutional or similar reasons the roll may be attacked.
[2] *Laws of Rhode Island, Title VIII*, chap. 46, sec. 15.
[3] *Laws of Virginia*, sec. 444.
[4] *Laws of West Virginia*, chap. 29, sec. 53.
[5] *Laws of Georgia*, sec. 839.

We turn now to the other phase of equalization. It was stated above that equalization of assessments must include the equalization of the valuations between the localities, i. e. between the local assessment areas—the towns or the townships of any particular county or between the various counties of the whole state. Equalization of this kind is provided for throughout the country.

The equalization of valuations in districts smaller than counties is of course limited to such states or counties within a state—where such districts are found. The county boards, in such cases, are given the authority to increase or decrease the valuation of any particular class of property or the aggregate valuation of property within any particular district. Usually, however, there is some provision which prevents the county board from increasing or decreasing the total valuation for the county beyond a prescribed percentage. Again, just as in the case of individuals a right of appeal is given, so in this case, a right of appeal from the decision of the county board is in some cases safeguarded to the town or district. In New York, for instance, appeal may be made to the State Board of Tax Commissioners [1] and in Iowa to the District Court.[2] In Michigan, however, the action of the county board is conclusive.[3]

For equalizing the valuation between the various counties most of the states have state boards of equalization. In about half of such states the "State Board of Equalization" is made up of various combinations of the regular executive officers of the state, while the other half have special boards.

[1] *Finance Law*, chap. 24, art. 8, sec. 174.
[2] *Laws of Iowa*, sec. 1375 *et seq.*
[3] *Laws of Michigan*, sec. 3857.

The combinations of the executive officers to form such state boards are many and only a few examples will be given. In Iowa, the Executive Council is the State Board of Equalization;[1] in Kansas we find the Secretary of State, the Auditor and the Treasurer making up the board;[2] in Missouri[3] and Montana,[4] the Governor, Auditor, Treasurer, Secretary of State and Attorney General; in South Dakota, the Governor, Auditor, Secretary of State, Treasurer and Commissioner of Schools[5] — and so on. The auditor, however, seems to be always included in such combinations.

The special boards which contain members other than or in addition to a number of the regular state executive officers are also variously made up. In California the Controller and one member elected from each congressional district constitute the state board.[6] Illinois' board is similarly constituted with the exception of the auditor or controller who is not found thereon.[7] In Indiana the State Board of Tax Commissioners is also the State Board of Equalization.[8] In Kentucky the board is composed of one member appointed from each appellate division by the Governor;[9] in Maine, of the State Board of Assessors;[10] in New Hampshire, of five members appointed by the Supreme Court;[11] in New Jersey, of five members appointed[12] by the

[1] *Laws of Iowa*, sec. 1378.
[2] *Laws of Kansas*, sec. 7608.
[3] *Constitution, Art. X*, sec. 18.
[4] *Laws of Montana*, sec. 3800.
[5] *Laws of South Dakota*, sec. 2109.
[6] *Political Code of California*, sec. 352.
[7] *Laws of Illinois*, chap. 120, sec. 100.
[8] *Laws of Indiana*, sec. 6384 *et seq.*
[9] *Laws of Kentucky*, sec. 4628.
[10] *Laws of Maine*, ch. 8, sec. 4.
[11] *Laws of New Hampshire*, ch. 63, sec. 1.
[12] *Laws of New Jersey*, 1905, ch. 67.

Governor and in Ohio—where there is a decennial board,— of one member elected from each senatorial district in the state.[1] In South Carolina one member is elected from each county board of equalization to serve on the state board.[2] In Minnesota the state board is made up of the Governor, Auditor and Attorney General and one qualified elector from each judicial district appointed by the Governor.[3]

As a general thing, it makes no great difference how the membership of such a board is made up, but it would seem better not to have the individual members represent only a county. Where there is a representative from each county each of such representatives feels it his duty to work for a low valuation for his own county rather than for a just equalization of the assessments between all the counties. Where, however, the members of a state board represent a larger area—such as a judicial or a congressional district— or where they are appointed for the state at large, they are not apt to feel such a strong local obligation and the probability is that the equalization will be more justly carried out.

It is, then, the duty of these state boards to equalize the valuation between the counties or, as in Maine, between the towns. They may, as a rule, require the attendance of assessors, may subpoena witnesses and are given, in general, the powers necessary for making careful examination of all matters that may bear upon the questions which they have to decide. They equalize the valuation by adding to or deducting from any class of property in the state as a whole or in any county a certain percentage of its valuation, or by adding to or deducting from the aggregate valuation in a county such percentage as may be necessary for equaliza-

[1] *Laws of Ohio*, sec. 2818. [2] *Laws of South Carolina*, sec. 388.
[3] *Laws of Minnesota*, sec. 1555.

tion. Sometimes a limit is put upon the change in the aggregate valuation of the property of the state that the board may make. In Colorado the board may not cause a variation in the aggregate valuation for the state of more than 10% and such variation may be only incidental to equalization.[1] Ten per cent is also the limit of variation in Idaho.[2] In North Dakota and Illinois the aggregate may not be reduced more than 1%.[3] In Minnesota no reduction at all may be made.[4] In South Dakota the board is forbidden to increase the valuation more than three millions of dollars.[5] In Nebraska instead of changing the valuation the board—which also determines the rate of the state tax—in order to equalize the assessment simply increases the rate of tax in each county which is undervalued.[6] In Kansas and New York the aggregate valuation may not be changed at all.[7]

When the entire process of equalization is completed it is the duty of the clerk or the secretary of the board to send a full notice of any change in the valuation of the property in any county to the county auditor or county clerk of such county. The county auditor or clerk—as the case may be—then adds to or deducts from the valuation of the property of each individual such percentage as the state board

[1] *Laws of Colorado*, Supplement, 1905, sec. 3927 v.
[2] *Laws of Idaho*, sec. 1385.
[3] *Laws of North Dakota*, sec. 1225. *Laws of Illinois*, chap. 120, sec. 100. Increase may not be more than 1% either. These restrictions do not apply to railroad property.
[4] *Laws of Minnesota*, 1897, ch. 134.
[5] This has been amended by ch. 65, *Laws of 1903*, so that the state board may now increase the valuation up to one hundred millions of dollars.
[6] *Laws of Nebraska*, sec. 4357.
[7] *Laws of Kansas*, sec. 7609. *Laws of New York, Finance Law*, ch. 24, art. 8, sec. 173. In New York this means simply that the aggregate valuation may not be reduced. It may, however, be increased.

may have added to or deducted from the entire county valuation.

It must be mentioned, however, that in some cases appeals from the decisions of the state board are provided for. In Kentucky for instance the County Judge of any county may appoint three persons to represent the county before the state board which must grant a rehearing and which may again change the valuation.[1] In Pennsylvania the counties may petition the common pleas court of Dauphin County for a rehearing.[2] In Wisconsin appeal lies to the circuit court.[3] But in most states it may be said that unless exception be taken on constitutional grounds, the action of the state board is final.

Levying the Tax: When the state board has finished its task of equalizing the assessments the determination of the amount of the state tax to be paid by each county is then made. The amount of the state tax to be levied on the entire property of the state is first determined. If the legislature has simply voted a certain rate to be levied on property there is nothing to do but have the auditor or controller or corresponding official certify the rate to the local officer in charge of assessments. Where the taxes are voted in dollars and cents it is possible for the state authorities to compute the rate on the basis of the entire state valuation, or the taxes may be apportioned to each county or town in proportion to valuation and the county and town authorities then given the task of computing the rate. Both means are employed. In Idaho, Iowa, Montana and Nebraska, for instance, the state board of equalization determines the rate; in Maine this duty devolves upon the state

---

[1] *Laws of Kentucky,* sec. 4274.
[2] *Laws of Pennsylvania,* col. 4114, sec. 7.
[3] *Laws of Wisconsin,* sec. 1077 a.

auditor; in Illinois upon the Governor, Auditor and Treasurer acting jointly; in Nebraska upon the Governor, Controller and Attorney General—and so on. In Kansas, Maine, Michigan, New Hampshire and some other states the taxes are first apportioned and the rates are computed by the local authorities. Oregon, however, has a scheme of apportionment that is decidedly unique. The Governor, Secretary of State and State Treasurer acting jointly compute from the various appropriations etc. of the legislature, the amount of revenue needed. Such amount is then apportioned among the counties—not according to the valuation of the property in the counties—but according to the proportion that the average amount of expenditures for the last five years in each county bears to the expenditure in all the counties. That is to say, the more any county spends on itself the larger becomes its share of the state taxes irrespective of the valuation of the property contained within its boundaries.

The final task is the determination, on the part of the local authorities, of the amount of taxes each individual must pay. In most of the states—except in New England where the town system prevails—the county authorities are given the task of collecting the taxes. The state taxes are certified to the county authorities and very general is the requirement that township, municipal, school district and other taxes regularly levied by properly constituted authorities be also certified to the county authorities. In New England, as has been said, the towns act independently in the matter. In both cases, however, the local authorities compute the rate or rates of taxation that must be levied on the property of each taxpayer, and the amounts computed to be due are then set down in a "tax roll" or "tax book" or "tax duplicate" opposite each individual's name. When the roll or duplicate is completed, the clerk or the auditor—

or whomsoever else is assigned to the duty of preparing the roll—then adds his affidavit to the effect that it is honestly and fully prepared and when all this has been done he sends it to the tax collector with a warrant attached directing the collector to collect the taxes as entered in the roll or duplicate. From the time the tax roll is put into the tax collector's hands the taxes become a first lien upon the property assessed. The real collection or the "gathering of the yield" then begins.

Collection: Just as with the assessment, so with the collection of the property tax the local authorities are most in evidence. A majority of the states make the county treasurers the ex-officio collectors in the counties. In some states [1] this duty devolves upon the county sheriff because the collection of a tax is often regarded as in the nature of the execution of a judgment. A few states—Alabama and Georgia for example—have specially appointed collectors in each county. The New England states, with their town systems, depend upon the town collectors, while some of the western states, where the township system is found, depend in like manner upon the township collector in the counties under township organization. Florida and Louisiana have regular state collectors who are looked upon as "state" rather than "county" or "parish" officials. These collectors, then, are charged with the duty of collecting the taxes which according to the assessment rolls or tax books are shown to be due from the various taxpayers of the district.

As a first step in the process the general requirement is that when the tax rolls are put into the hands of the collector he must in some way give notice to the various tax-

[1] Arkansas, Illinois, Kentucky, North Carolina, Oregon and West Virginia.

payers that their taxes are due and that such taxes can be paid at certain times and places. Very often the collector must publish such notice in a newspaper for a prescribed time or he must post a given number of notices at conspicuous places in the town or the county where it can be reasonably supposed that they will come to the attention of the taxpayers. In some states — Colorado for example — notices are sent to the taxpayers by mail. In Wyoming postal-card notices are sent to all taxpayers three days before their taxes become delinquent warning them to pay their taxes before these become delinquent.[1] In one way or another the attempt is thus made to give each taxpayer sufficient notice of his indebtedness to the state in order that he may as expeditiously as possible remove the same by paying his taxes.

All of the states require the taxpayers to come to the tax collector to pay their taxes. A few states [2] do require that the tax collector make a personal demand on those owing for taxes just after such taxes have become delinquent, but as penalties are levied on delinquents, the penalty may be considered as a species of compensation to the state for the additional trouble caused the collector. A majority of the states in which the collection is undertaken by the county officers, require,—for the convenience of taxpayers living at a distance from the county seat—that the collector or his deputy attend for a specified period in each " election precinct " or " justice's district " or similar minor division of the county, to collect the taxes in such district. But in the other states no special arrangement of this kind is found. In the latter, taxpayers must betake themselves to the office of the collector to pay their tax bills.

[1] *Laws of Wyoming*, sec. 1868.
[2] Alabama, Michigan, New Jersey and Wyoming, for example.

The laws of each state prescribe when the taxes are due. As a rule a definite period of time is specified during which the taxes may be paid. These periods are not the same from state to state but vary from about two weeks to two months, and a distinction is frequently made between personalty insecured by real estate, personalty so secured and real estate, in fixing them. In some states, indeed, (California for example) the assessor himself may demand immediate payment of taxes on all personal property insufficiently secured by real estate and may even seize it and sell it for such taxes if necessary. This happens rarely, however, because such property is not extensively reached any way.

As an inducement to taxpayers to pay their taxes early some states allow a rebate or discount on the amount due. Oregon, for instance, allows a rebate of 3% if the taxes are paid about a month before the expiration of the period during which they are considered regularly due.[1] West Virginia allows a rebate of 2½%.[2] Kansas allows a rebate of 5% on half the amount of the taxes if the whole amount is paid when the first half is due.[3] Maryland allows a rebate of 5% or 4% or 3% according as the taxes are paid respectively 3 months, 2 months or 1 month before they become delinquent.[4] In Michigan the rebate is allowed in a different form.[5] Taxes there become delinquent on March 1st. On all taxes that are paid between January 10th and the date of delinquency a collection charge of 4% is levied; but on taxes voluntarily paid before January 10th the collection charge is only 1%. It is also to be noted that a

[1] *Laws of Oregon*, sec. 3106
[2] *Laws of West Virginia*, ch. 30, sec. 6.
[3] *Laws of Kansas*, sec. 7621.   [4] *Laws of Maryland*, art. 81.
[5] *Michigan Laws*, sec. 3867.

considerable number of states [1] allow the property taxes to be paid in two installments, at intervals of about six months, in order that the burden may not weigh too heavily on the taxpayer at any one time.

If the taxes are not paid when they are due they become delinquent and the persons upon whom the legal responsibility of payment rests are known as "delinquents." Usually a very considerable penalty is imposed on delinquents, although, as is to be expected, some states deal less harshly with them than do others. Interest is practically always charged on overdue taxes and in most of the states a penalty is added. These penalties are as a rule in the form of a percentage addition to the taxes. Thus in Ohio and Virginia, for example, a penalty of 5% on the amount due is affixed; in Kentucky such penalty is 6%; in Wyoming, 8%; in a number of states [2] it is 10% while in Iowa, Colorado and Tennessee it amounts to 1% a month. South Dakota levies a penalty of 1% after the first month, 2% after the second month and so on, besides a rate of interest of 1% a month. In South Carolina and Washington the penalty is 15%. In California the penalty is 15% and five months later an additional 5% is charged. In North Dakota a penalty of 5% is charged on delinquent personalty and interest at the rate of 1% a month, while on real estate, the original penalty is 3% and a month later an additional 3% is charged and three months after that an additional 3% and five months after that an additional 5% is added. In some states the interest charged is at a rate so high that it may be considered to contain an appreciable punitive element,[3] whereas in a few of the states mentioned above no

[1] California, Colorado, Indiana, Iowa, Kansas, Nevada, Ohio, Oregon, South Dakota and Washington.
[2] Idaho, Indiana, Minnesota, Montana, Nevada, Nebraska and Oregon.
[3] Kansas, for instance, where the rate is 10%.

interest is charged in addition to the penalty which is itself considered sufficient. In all of the states, however, after a varying length of time, if the overdue taxes are not paid, the property of the delinquent is seized upon and sold at public auction according to rules prescribed by law.[1]

In the seizure of the property of delinquents, movable property is always taken first but if there should not be enough of that, the real estate of such delinquent is also seized upon and sold. Personalty once sold is practically forever gone but the law always provides for the redemption of real property by the original owner (i. e. by him from whom it was taken) or by any one else having an interest in it. Such redemption must, however, be made within a limited period of two or three years in fairness to the purchaser who then demands that he be given a clear and unobstructed title. At best such redemption is a very costly process for the one who undertakes it. Thus it is seen that although the state often steps in and saves an unfortunate debtor from having all of his property taken by his creditors who may have just claims against him, still, in levying its own charges no consideration is allowed to stand in the way of a full liquidation of such charge when once it has been legally imposed. The state's lien for taxes is always a first lien and therefore one that must be satisfied before all others.

(2) *The Property Tax on Miscellaneous Corporations:*[2]

The property of what we have called miscellaneous cor-

[1] The authorities for each state for the statements made in the above paragraph have not been given, as any one of them may be verified by consulting the code of laws of the state and looking in the index of the same under the head of "Delinquency."

[2] In the group of miscellaneous corporations are considered those other than the so-called "quasi-public" corporations and banks, which, in the majority of cases, are separately provided for. The quasi-public corporations and banks will be separately referred to.

porations is in every state of the Union taxed in one form or another. The differences that arise from state to state are due to the various kinds of efforts put forth to reach all of the property of a corporation. The departure from the strict theory of the property tax in states like New York was due not to a disbelief in the theory so much as to the inability to reach all the property according to that theory.

The constitutions of some ten states [1] provide that the property of corporations shall be taxed in the same way as that of individuals but in a great majority of the states without such constitutional provisions the property of corporations is nevertheless so taxed. The points of interest that arise in this connection have to do simply with the methods employed in reaching and assessing all such property.

The real estate of corporations is everywhere taxed in the same way as is the real estate of individuals.[2] Corporate real estate is listed to the corporation and is assessed by the local authorities. The valuation of such real estate is equalized in exactly the same way as is the valuation of the real estate of individuals and in all other respects the treatment is practically the same. It is in regard to personalty—tangible and intangible—that the differences arise.

In a few of the states — Colorado and Montana for example—no distinction is made between tangible and intangible property in the process of listing but each corporation is listed as a business unit. The whole plant is considered as a unit and the determination of its value is based upon a consideration of the realty and the personalty and

---

[1] Alabama, Idaho, Iowa, Kentucky, Mississippi, Nevada, Ohio, South Carolina, Utah and Washington.

[2] We are not considering here the special corporations.

all the franchise privileges. Then in other of the states [1] the realty and personalty of the corporation are both locally assessed and no special effort is made to reach the intangible property. At least two-thirds of the states do, however, have special provisions for reaching all intangible property.

This special provision for reaching intangible property has for the most part taken the form of a tax on capital stock. This tax is assessed in various ways. In all cases the valuation is based on a statement made to the local or state assessing officers, giving under oath detailed information concerning the property, capital stock, earnings, etc., of each corporation. Such valuation is more commonly made by the local assessor although in some half dozen of the states the duty devolves upon the state officers.[2] From such statements the assessing authorities determine the value of the entire capital stock of the plant, although they are, of course, given the right to examine the books, etc., of the corporation. From the aggregate value so determined there is deducted the assessed value of the realty and tangible personalty and such indebtedness as may be allowed, although in some states [3] the assessed value of realty alone is deducted and such tangible personal property as there may be is then not subject to separate taxation. Here again the assessing authority need not accept the valuation as given in the statement. Sometimes the law lays down a rule as to what factors the assessor shall take into account in deter-

[1] Arkansas, California, Idaho, Kentucky, Louisiana, Missouri and Washington.

[2] Illinois, Maryland, Massachusetts, North Carolina, Pennsylvania, and Texas. In Illinois the assessing authority is the State Board of Equalization; in Indiana, Maryland and Massachusetts, the state tax commissioners.

[3] Maryland, Massachusetts, Rhode Island, Vermont, West Virginia, and maybe a few others.

mining the valuation but it always places upon him the duty of making such a determination himself.

The assessment thus made is subject to review. In the states where there is the assessment by the local authorities there is the usual review by the local boards of equalization. In the states where the assessment is by state officers certain special means of appeal are provided for or otherwise the corporations are allowed to go to the courts. In Maryland for example appeal may be taken to the comptroller and treasurer. If they are both of one opinion the assessment that they make stands but if either agrees with the tax commissioner (the original assessing authority) the latter's assessment stands.[1] In Massachusetts appeal may be made to a Board of Appeal—and so on.

The rate of the tax is also determined in most cases as is the rate on the property of individuals. In Massachusetts, however, the rate is determined by the average rate of all taxation—state and local—upon the assessed value of all the property in the state. In New York, the rate is fixed by law and varies according as the dividends are above or below 6%.[2] In Pennsylvania also the earnings principle is employed. As a general thing, however, the intangible personalty, after it has once been assessed is dealt with as any other kind of property and bears its proportion of the various state and local rates.

The capital stock so assessed is, in most cases, assessed directly to the corporation although in some states[3] the assessment is made against the stockholders while the corporation pays all or a part of the tax. It seems to be the custom in some of the New England states to make the re-

[1] *Laws of Maryland*, art. 81, sec. 144.

[2] *Finance Law*, ch. 24, art. ix, sec. 182.

[3] Alabama, Iowa, New Hampshire, Rhode Island, Maryland, Maine, and Vermont.

sident shareholders responsible for the taxes on their holdings while the corporation itself is held responsible for the taxes on the shares of non-residents.[1] In the states where the corporations pay the taxes for the shareholders a full list of the shareholders must be made out for the assessing authorities. The corporation after paying the taxes may deduct the amount of the same from the dividends and it has also a lien on the shares of stock to the amount of such taxes.

The taxes are payable in some states to the local collecting authorities and in others like New York and Massachusetts they are paid directly into the state treasury. Where they are paid to the local authorities the periods of payment etc. conform generally to those fixed for the taxes on other property, and where they are paid directly into the state treasury the time of payment is specially fixed by law. Interest and penalties for delinquency are also provided. Money fines are levied if the required statements are not seasonably submitted, the corporation is fined for delinquency in payment of taxes and interest is charged on taxes overdue. Shares of stock and the property of corporations may also be seized and sold if the tax is not ultimately paid, just as the property of individuals is dealt with under similar circumstances.

(3) *The Tax on the Property of Certain Special Corporations:*

Banks and Banking Companies: The property of banks has been almost uniformly regarded with peculiar jealousy and special efforts have been made to insure the listing of all bank property for taxation. The methods employed in assessing bank property are exceptionally uniform throughout the states as a result of certain United States Supreme

---

[1] Maine, New Hampshire, Rhode Island, and Vermont.

Court decisions and the general success of the scheme employed. The shares of banks are one of the few kinds of personal property that bear their full burden of taxation.

The real estate of the banks is assessed in all respects as is the real estate of individuals so that no particular attention need be given to such assessment.

The shares of stock of incorporated banks,—state and national—are assessed almost uniformly as the personal property of the owners at the place where the bank is located. For purposes of assessment the president or the cashier of the bank must make out a sworn statement of the capital stock of the company, par and market value of same, surplus and undivided profits, property, etc. and a full list of the stockholders with their residences, holdings, etc. This statement is delivered to the local assessor, whose duty it is then to determine the assessable value of such shares. He is given the power to examine the bank's books, subpoena witnesses, etc. in his endeavor to get at all the facts that are relevant to such valuation. Sometimes the law declares what factors are to be considered in the determination of such assessable value. In New York, for instance, the value of the capital is considered to be made up of the amount of the capital stock, the surplus and the undivided profits. When the valuation of the entire capital is made the assessed value of the bank's realty is deducted, and the remainder divided by the number of shares gives the value at which each share is assessed. In states where deductions for debt are allowed to be made from the assessed value of " moneyed capital " the same allowance is made in regard to bank shares; that is to say, an individual shareholder in such states may have deductions made from the assessed value of his bank holdings for such amount of his bona-fide indebtedness as the laws of his state may provide in the case of other moneyed capital.

The right to appeal the assessment so made is usually provided. Such appeal lies in most cases to the local board of equalization or to the courts. In Ohio, however, the Governor, Auditor and Attorney General form a special board of appeal.[1]

Against the value assessed the regular taxes are levied and the bank is responsible for the payment of the same to the local authorities. For the taxes so paid, however, the bank has a lien against the stock itself and it may deduct the amount of such taxes from the dividends.

The general plan outlined above for the assessment of banks is by far the most common method employed. There are, of course, certain variations from this general method, a few of which may be referred to. In Iowa, for instance, the shares of state banks and trust companies instead of being assessed to the shareholders are assessed to the corporation itself.[2] In Kentucky, again, the assessment of the shares of national banks is by state officers—Auditor, Treasurer and Secretary of State—and the state tax is paid directly into the state treasury.[3] In Maryland, Massachusetts, North Carolina and Pennsylvania also the taxes for the state are paid directly into the state treasury. Then in the New England states[4] and one or two others, the bank, instead of paying the tax on the shares of all the stockholders, pays the tax on the shares of non-residents only. Each bank must send to the town or other local assessors a statement showing the number of shareholders residing in such town or other local district and the amount of their holdings, for the taxes upon which such residents

---

[1] *Laws of Ohio*, sec. 2808.   [2] *Laws of Iowa*, sec. 1322.

[3] *Laws of Kentucky*, 1904—"Act for providing for the assessment of the shares of capital of national banks."

[4] Maine, New Hampshire, New Jersey, Rhode Island and Vermont.

are then held personally liable. Finally it may be said that in New York there is a fixed rate of 1% on the assessed value of the shares.[1]

Penalties for delinquency and interest on the taxes overdue are of course uniformly provided and the payment of the taxes due can be enforced by the seizure and sale of the stock itself. Considered as a whole, however, there is probably less friction and less trouble in the collection of these taxes than in the collection of any other portion of the property tax.

Quasi-Public Corporations: The growth of the public service corporation introduced another difficulty in the operation of the general property tax. These quasi-public organizations dependent upon public franchises or privileges of one kind or another, which as population advanced became always more and more valuable, had early to be subjected to special methods of inquisition and valuation in order that they might bear at least an approximately just share of the public burden.

Various attempts were made with this end in view. In general the process was one of centralization in financial administration — a centralization that seems destined to continue in its various phases as the great corporations of all kinds widen ever more their operations. The wonderful centralization that has been going on in all our political life can, indeed, find a very large measure of its explanation in the industrial expansion that has characterized our history since the Civil War. Foremost in this industrial expansion come the great railroads and other quasi-public corporations which have leaped beyond the mere boundaries of county and state and of even the nation itself and which seem to be limited in their growth only by insuperable natural

---

[1] *Laws of New York*, 1901, ch. 550.

barriers and the prospects of trade. It is because of their pre-eminent position in this field of industrial expansion that the tendency toward centralized control in financial and other matters has been most marked in connection with such quasi-public corporations and that is why it becomes of more than ordinary interest to consider them at this place.

In a large majority of the states these corporations that we have in mind — namely the railroad, telegraph, telephone, sleeping-car, express, tank-line, fast-freight, pipe-line, etc., corporations—are still subject to the general property tax. Various modifications of, and additions to, the theory of the general property tax can, of course, be found from state to state;—in New York for instance the tax is frankly abandoned for state purposes and a tax based upon earnings is substituted—but these modifications interest us here only in a general way. Our purpose at this point is to give some account of the means employed in those states where the property tax is still in vogue, for arriving at a just estimate of the value of the property upon which these various corporations should be taxed.

Assessment: The assessment of such corporate property is generally entrusted to a single state board. As in Iowa, for example, the Executive Council is the assessing body for railways, as well as telegraph, telephone, etc. companies, so in most of the other states similar boards are entrusted with the same powers. Of course, there are various departures from this rule. In Ohio, for example, the assessment of the property of each railroad company is entrusted to a board composed of the auditors of the counties through which such company's lines extend,[1] while the other corporations are assessed by a State Board of Appraisers and Assessors composed of the State Auditor,

---

[1] *Laws of Ohio*, sec. 2770 *et seq.*

Treasurer and Attorney General.[1] In general however the rule holds good and no attempt will be made to point out the exceptions.

This board is, in about half the states, the State Board of Equalization. In a few others—Tennessee for example—it is composed of the railway commissioners. In Vermont on the other hand, the Tax Commissioner is the assessing authority.[2] In Virginia the Corporation Commission[3] and in West Virginia the Board of Public Works acts in the capacity referred to;[4] in Wisconsin the Tax Commissioner and the first and second assistants.[5] In Georgia the Comptroller General on the statement of the local authorities determines the assessment upon which the state tax is levied.[6] In Florida the Comptroller acts with the advice and consent of the Treasurer and the Attorney General.[7] In Kansas the Lieutenant-Governor, Secretary of State, Treasurer, Auditor and Attorney General form a State Board of Assessors.[8] In Kentucky the assessment is made by the Railroad Commission.[9] In Texas the assessing board is composed of the Comptroller, Secretary of State and Tax Commissioner.[10] In these various ways then, is the assessing authority, for railroads and similar corporations, constituted.

It must be noted, however, that in a few states [11] the as-

---

[1] *Supra*, sec. 2778.
[2] *Laws of Vermont*, sec. 547 *et seq.*
[3] See Constitution of Virginia.
[4] *Laws of West Virginia*, 1905, ch. 35.
[5] *Laws of Wisconsin*, 1903, ch. 315.
[6] *Laws of Georgia*, sec. 779 *et seq.*
[7] *Laws of Florida*, title 6, ch. 1, sec. 376.
[8] *Laws of Kansas*, sec. 7551 *et seq.*
[9] *Laws of Kentucky*, sec. 4096.
[10] See Laws of 1905.
[11] Oregon and Nevada.

sessment is chiefly in the hands of the local authorities, while in such states as have done away with the general property tax on these corporations for state purposes, the realty and tangible personalty is nevertheless assessable by the local authorities for local purposes. In some states also the realty and tangible personal property is locally assessed while "franchise" or "capital stock" is assessed by the state authorities. Distinctions of this kind are however too numerous to warrant our considering them in detail here.

In all cases there is required as the first step in the process of valuation a sworn statement from a responsible officer of the company. These statements vary somewhat according to the particular kind of business to which they refer (i. e. railroad, telegraph, express, etc.) and they are more or less comprehensive and detailed as the laws of the several states and the regulations of the assessing authorities may determine. The uniform aim is to get an adequate collection of facts according to which the value of the property, or the base upon which the tax is to be levied, may be determined.

The details of these statements as was stated above, differ according to the character of the business but as an example that may be considered more or less typical of all of them, there can be given an outline of the statement required by the laws of Iowa to be made out for the Executive Council by railroad companies.[1] Iowa was chosen purely at random.

1. Whole number of miles of railway owned, operated or leased, within and without the state. 2. Whole number of miles owned, etc., within the state including double and side tracks,—mileage of main lines and branch lines to be stated separately—and showing the number of miles of

[1] *Laws of Iowa*, sec. 1334 *et seq.*

track in each county. (For telegraph and telephone companies these points would have to do with wire mileage and the number of poles, etc., while for sleeping-car, express, etc., companies, car-mileage or miles of line over which the companies operate would be required). 3. Detailed statements showing real estate in each county including right-of-way, roadbed, etc. and estimated value thereof. 4. A full statement of the cost and actual present value of all buildings of every description owned by said railway company not otherwise assessed. 5. Total number of ties per mile within the state. 6. Weight of rails per yard in main line, double tracks and side tracks. 7. Number of miles of telegraph lines owned and used within the state. 8. Total number of engines; passenger, freight, etc., cars, and number of each class in the state, each class being valued separately. 9. Any and all other movable property classified as the Executive Council may determine. 10. Gross earnings of entire road and gross earnings in state. 11. Operating expenses of entire road and operating expenses in state. 12. Net earnings of entire road and net earnings in state.[1] Usually also, a detailed statement of the financial organization of the company is required—the amount of the capital stock, the number of shares, a statement of dividends declared for specified periods in the past, the par and market value of the shares, the highest price paid for shares during the year past and also the lowest price in the market operations, a detailed statement of the bonded indebtedness, etc. Very often also the law explains carefully what the various subdivisions shall contain. The railways, for example, are fond of including improvements in operating expenses, so that in a considerable number of states the law prescribes what may be considered operating expenses: or

[1] *Laws of Iowa*, sec. 1334.

at least what may not be so considered.[1] These are, however, some of the finer points that cannot be taken up within the limits of this treatise.

These statements made under oath by a responsible officer of the company concerned constitute, then, the basis upon which the valuation of the company's property is made. In no case, however, need the assessing authority limit itself to this statement. Just as the local assessor may interrogate and examine the individual so the authority assessing the property of these corporations may examine their books, subpoena officers and witnesses and thus attempt to discover for itself the various facts requisite for a just estimate of their property.

The factors to be considered in such valuation sometimes are and sometimes are not prescribed. In some states the assessing authorities are allowed to determine for themselves the principles according to which the valuation is to be made while in others the process of determining the valuation is set down in the law or emphasis is at least laid upon certain considerations that from the standpoint of the law are especially important. In Kansas for instance the state board may assess the various properties "as it deems just,"[2] while a few examples—having to do mostly with railroad property—may be given to illustrate the opposite tendency. In Iowa the law specifically directs that the gross earnings per mile are to be considered in assessing value.[3] In North Carolina the law directs that the Corporation Commission shall first determine the value of the tangible property of each division or branch of railway and directs further that, in this connection, the cost of replace-

[1] See, for example, *Laws of Iowa*, sec. 1335.
[2] *Laws of Kansas*, sec. 7557.
[3] *Laws of Iowa*, sec. 1336.

ment and depreciation are to be considered. It directs the Commission in the next place to assess the value of the franchise—such value to be determined by due consideration of gross earnings as compared with the operating expenses and particularly by consideration of the value placed upon the whole property by the public (the value of the physical property being deducted) as evidenced by the market value of the capital stock, certificates of indebtedness, etc., the value of which is based upon earning capacity. The aggregate value of the tangible property and the franchise is then to be the true value for ad-valorem taxation.[1] In South Carolina the Board is directed to determine the true cash value of the whole property first and the rule is laid down that the market or actual value of the entire capital stock together with the aggregate amount of mortgages or liens shall be deemed the true cash value.[2] Texas has a similar provision.[3]

The most interesting point in this connection, however, depends upon the fact that most of these corporations are corporations engaged in interstate trade. The various lines of railway, telegraph, etc., companies go beyond the bounds of a single state and consequently they are liable for taxation in any particular state only on such part of their property as can be rightly considered to be within such state. This introduces a host of difficulties and throws upon the assessing authority in each state the nice task of determining what share of the property of each of such corporations is to be taxed in the state concerned.

Here it becomes necessary to distinguish more particularly between the different classes of corporations owing to the differences in the nature of their businesses.

[1] *Laws of North Carolina*, 1905, ch. 590.
[2] *Laws of South Carolina*, sec. 294.
[3] Laws of 1905.

For railways the most common principle employed in apportioning the value of the entire property as estimated by the assessing authority is that of mileage. This principle is based on the theory that, considering the railroad as an organized whole, the value mile for mile is about the same. An average value per mile is thus determined and such average multiplied by the number of miles of line in the state gives the valuation that is made the basis of the assessment. In some cases allowance is made for especially good terminal facilities or for considerations of similar import in other states, but this is not the general practice. Whether the average value per mile is determined or not it may be said that, in regard to railroads, the proportion of the value of any corporation's property taxable in a particular state is determined by the ratio of the mileage of the company's lines in such state to the entire mileage within and without the state. The very general practice is to include in such apportionment only such property as is used in the railway business itself—property that would in any event be considered an integral part of the business—while other property, owned by the railway company but not directly used in connection with its business, is locally assessed.

The property of telephone and telegraph companies is similarly apportioned according to wire mileage in each state. Either the average value of the property per mile of wire is determined and the mileage in the state used as a multiplier or an apportionment of the value of the property as a whole based on the proportion of total wire mileage in the state is made, to determine what amount of the company's property is taxable in any particular state. In a few of the states [1] there is still the simple property tax locally

[1] Montana, Nevada, Oregon, Washington and West Virginia.

assessed and in a few other states [1] the tax on the property of these companies takes the form of an arbitrary rate per mile of wire or per instrument, in which case, of course, the theory of the property tax is departed from and an apportionment of the value of the property as a whole is obviously unnecessary.

In the apportionment of the valuation of the property of sleeping-car, express, fast-freight lines and similar companies somewhat different principles are employed.

The most common method of apportioning the property of sleeping-car companies is on the basis of the mileage of lines over which a company operates within and without the state. That is to say, the ratio of the mileage over which the company operates within a state to the entire mileage over which the company operates determines the proportion of its property which is taxable in such state. This method is employed in some seventeen states.[2] In some of these states, however, all realty and tangible personalty is locally assessed and the apportionment refers only to the assessed value of the " franchise " or the " capital stock " in all of which cases allowance is made of course for the property locally assessed.

Another method employed in apportioning such valuation is based on the mileage actually made by the company's cars rather than the miles of line over which the company operates. In Missouri,[3] for example, sleeping-car and similar companies have to make the usual annual report, including a statement of the mileage made by their cars in

[1] California, Connecticut, Mississippi and Texas.

[2] Arkansas, Georgia, Indiana, Kentucky, Colorado, Louisiana, Massachusetts, Michigan, North Carolina, North Dakota, Ohio, Oregon, South Carolina, South Dakota, Texas, Virginia, Wisconsin and Wyoming.

[3] *Laws of Missouri*, sec. 9345.

the state and the average mileage per day of the cars of the particular class covered by the statement. The railroad companies must also furnish a mileage statement for whatever number of such cars they may have used. The state board then takes the average mileage per day of cars of each class and divides the total mileage of the cars of each class by such average mileage and the quotient represents the number of the cars of each class that are estimated to have been necessary to make the total mileage and upon such number of cars is the assessment based.[1] In Nebraska on the other hand, the method employed is based on monthly averages.[2] The railway companies must in the first instance report the number of sleeping, etc. cars used during each month of the year for which the statement is made and also the number of miles each month such cars have been run on such railway and the total mileage each car made within and without the state. The law further provides that the average number of such cars used by such railway corporation each month and the assessed value of said cars shall bear the same proportion to the entire value thereof that the monthly average number of miles that the cars have been run in the state shall bear to the monthly average number of miles that said cars have been run within and without the state.

In most of the other states not already referred to the property of the sleeping-car and similar companies is assessed by the local authorities although there are in addition privilege taxes, license taxes or taxes on gross receipts. A word will be said about these taxes later, so that further consideration of them may be waived at this point.

Express companies are assessed on their property in

[1] *Laws of Missouri*, sec. 9348.
[2] *Laws of Nebraska*, sec. 4322.

about half the states by the state authorities,[1] although in some of these states—just as in the case of sleeping, etc. car companies,—the real estate and the tangible personalty may be locally assessed. Where there is assessment of the whole or a part of the property by the state authorities the basis of the apportionment is uniformly the mileage of the lines over which a company operates. This is obviously the only practicable method since the express companies do a large part of their business in the cars owned by the railway companies. In the other half of the states there is, as has been said, a local assessment of real estate and tangible personalty while the state levies simply an arbitrary license or privilege tax or a percentage tax on gross receipts.

Most states assess the property of fast-freight and similar companies in about the same way as they do express companies. The apportionment of the valuation when the assessment is made by the state authorities, is for the most part according to mileage operated over within and without the state. In Colorado [2] and Iowa,[3] however, the apportionment is based simply on the mileage actually made by the cars of a company, within and without the state. In Kansas each company's statement — which is supplemented by one from the railroads—must show the aggregate number of car-days made by its cars on the several lines of railroad in the state during the year which the statement covers, and also the total number of cars owned. The Board of Railway Assessors divides the total number of car-days so ascertained by the number of days in the preceding year and the quotient so obtained constitutes the

[1] About the same states that were referred to in connection with sleeping-car companies.
[2] *Laws*, Supp. 1905, sec. 3917.
[3] *Laws.* Supp. 1902, sec. 1342 D.

number of cars on which the company is assessed. A carday represents each day that a car is used or operated in the state. In other words, the average number of cars used in the state during the preceding year is, in Kansas, made the basis of the assessment and the valuation represents the average cash value of such average number of cars for each class.[1] The same system is in vogue in Michigan.[2] In Wyoming the assessment is based on the average number of cars used as determined by the average mileage per day of the cars of each class compared with the total mileage for the year—just as in Missouri the assessment of sleeping-car companies is made.[3]

In the other states, not already referred to in this connection, there is simply the local assessment of the property of these corporations by the local authorities,[4] or there are in addition to such local assessments, " privilege " taxes or taxes based on receipts and earnings.[5]

Equalization: In determining the valuation of the property of these various classes of quasi-public corporations they are as a rule given the right to be heard. Each company is given an opportunity to explain its statement to the assessing authority and to make whatever plea in connection therewith that it sees fit. In a good many cases when the valuation has been once fixed such valuation is final although in some states a rehearing is specifically provided for.[6] In Colorado after the valuation has been fixed a

[1] *Laws of Kansas*, 1905, ch. 500.
[2] *Laws of Michigan*, 1905, no. 282.
[3] *Laws of Wyoming*, 1901, ch. 81.
[4] Montana, Nevada, Washington, Idaho, California, South Dakota, Tennessee, Connecticut and New Hampshire.
[5] Marylan , New Jersey, New York, Pennsylvania and Vermont.
[6] A suit at law on constitutional grounds is, of course, always possible.

company feeling itself aggrieved may, within a prescribed time, file a petition of complaint with the Governor.[1] The Governor calls a meeting of the State Board and the complaints are heard. In Kentucky, Mississippi and Montana also the companies may appeal for a rehearing and in Wisconsin and Wyoming a similar right of review is provided. In other states an action at law is provided for.[2] In Tennessee the Governor, Treasurer and Secretary of State form a special board of equalization for railway, telegraph and telephone property.[3] Where there is simply the local assessment the methods of review are those employed in the case of other property. In Ohio, however, where railways are assessed by boards composed of the county auditors, as was explained above, there is a special board of equalization composed of the Auditor of State, Treasurer, and Commissioner of Railroads and Telegraph.[4] When the valuation has been finally determined the next task that presents itself has to do with fixing the rate to be levied on such valuation.

Determination of the Tax: The methods employed in calculating the rate are various. The most common method is to apportion the entire valuation, as fixed by the Board, among the smaller political divisions in proportion to mileage of lines for railway, telegraph and telephone companies and in proportion to mileage operated upon for the other companies. In such cases the local authorities are charged with the duty of computing the various taxes due on such property in exactly the same way as they do on the property

[1] *Laws of Colorado*, Supplement, 1905, sec. 3899.
[2] Georgia, Louisiana, New Hampshire, New Jersey, and West Virginia.
[3] *Laws of Tennessee*, Supp. 1897-1903, sec. 824-859.
[4] *Laws of Ohio*, sec. 2871.

of individuals. Similarly where there is at the outset only a local assessment the local authorities compute the various amounts due. But in some states where the assessment of all or a part of the property of these corporations is made by the state authorities, these same authorities compute the taxes to be levied on such property for state purposes.[1] Ordinarily the rate is simply the general state rate on all property while the local rates are separately levied, but in some four of the states [2] the attempt is made to levy the average rate of all taxes levied on other property throughout the state. In Michigan, for instance, the proper local authorities must send in to the state authorities full records of the assessed valuation of all property and of all taxes levied upon such property within their respective jurisdictions. These are then totaled for the whole state and the average rate is determined by dividing the total taxes by the total valuation. In Michigan this tax is in lieu of all other state and local taxes except special assessments. In the other three states referred to a similar determination is made.[3]

Collection: However then the rate be determined—by the state or by the local authorities — the amount chargeable to each company is calculated. This amount is then certified by the proper authority to the company charged with the tax and within the time prescribed by law the tax must

---

[1] California, Florida, Georgia, Massachusetts, Michigan, New Hampshire, North Carolina, Tennessee, Virginia, West Virginia and Wisconsin for the property of railroads and most of the other quasi-public corporations.

Missouri and Ohio for that of car companies, and Nebraska for that of express, steamboat and other transportation companies, excepting street-car companies.

[2] Massachusetts, Michigan, New Hampshire and Wisconsin.

[3] *Laws of Michigan*, 1905, no. 282, sec. 12.

be paid. And without going into detail it may be said that just as in the case of individuals penalties are inflicted for delinquency and interest is charged, so with these big corporations heavy penalties are levied upon delinquents, interest is charged on the taxes overdue and their property may be seized and sold if the taxes are not ultimately paid.

(4) *Critical Remarks:*

It would seem hardly necessary in this place to say much by way of criticism of the general property tax as employed in our states. This tax has been so generally criticized by writers on Finance that the merest tyro in the subject in this country is familiar with most of its defects. To some extent, therefore, our efforts here may constitute a work of supererogation but they will at least serve the purpose of emphasizing some of the criticisms from the point of view of this chapter.

Here we are not concerned with the theory of the property tax although that itself is unsound. We are concerned only with the realization of this theory in practice. In other words we have to deal only with the means employed for collecting the tax. But in this connection it must be said that the weightiest and most numerous criticisms that have been brought against the property tax relate to this very question of administration.

The most comprehensive and thorough criticism of the general property tax is to be found in Professor E. R. A. Seligman's " Essays in Taxation." As a matter of fact there is nothing left for anybody else to do except to add more and later illustrations to clinch what is already an invincible argument. Therefore it is frankly admitted that no originality is aimed at in this place, the sole aim being to show as briefly as possible how from beginning to end the administration of the general property tax is saturated with error and injustice.

The first great criticism that must be brought against the administration of the tax is that under our political conditions it is practically impossible to assess the tax uniformly. The law requires that all property be assessed at "fair cash value" or "market value." It is sometimes provided that only a percentage of such value be taken as the assessed valuation, but as this applies uniformly throughout the state that fact itself has no particular significance. The cash or market value must in any case be first determined. In all cases the local assessor is under oath to carry out the provisions of the law in the process of valuation and his general oath is usually buttressed by special oaths before and after the actual process of valuation is undertaken and completed. But here, right at the outset, the administration fails. The assessors voluntarily or under political compulsion forget and violate their oaths. Partizanship and other causes lead to glaring injustice in the assessment of the property of individuals in the same assessment district and the desire to ingratiate themselves into the favor of their constituents leads the assessors to vie with each other in bringing down the general valuation of their districts as far as possible. As Professor Seligman points out, the "official reports abound with complaints and open confessions that property is assessed all the way from par to one twenty-fifth of the actual value."[1]

The report[2] of the Committee on Double Taxation in Vermont shows that the assessors in the towns frankly admitted that they had entered the assessed value of property from 66⅔% to 100% of the true value upon which they had promised under oath to make the assessment. The injus-

[1] *Essays in Taxation*, p. 25.   [2] Made in 1900; see page 35.

tice here involved is supposed to be remedied by subsequent equalization, but the further removed from the local districts these tribunals of equalization are the more difficult does it become for them to equalize valuations in a degree even approximating uniformity. In the assessment of railroad and similar property the difficulty is obviated somewhat by having the state assessing boards as was shown above—but it is notorious that such property is not assessed on as high a basis as is other property in general throughout the states. The sinister influence of the corporations has been too strong in the central state boards. It may be said then that the first great canon of just taxation—that requiring a tax to be uniform throughout the area in which it is applied—is violated at the very beginning in the administration of the general property tax.

The second great criticism that must be brought against the administration of the general property tax in the states is that it is not equally assessed on persons liable to the tax. Every state in the Union requires persons in legal possession of taxable property to list the same for taxation. In New York for example there is found the broad requirement that assessors ascertain the names of taxable persons and their property.[1] In Ohio the law requires "every person of full age and sound mind" to list his property.[2] In Indiana the law requires the assessor to call upon each and every person in the township for a list.[3] But here again the assessors generally are forgetful of their oaths and in not a few cases it is impossible for them to carry out the provisions of the law. In the rural districts where population is sparse not many can escape the assessor but in the

[1] *Laws of New York*, ch. 24, art. 11, sec. 20.
[2] *Laws of Ohio*, sec. 2734.
[3] *Laws of Indiana*, sec. 6358.

cities it is impossible for the assessor to discover all those that are taxable and it is equally impossible for him to call in person on each and every person in his district and require such person to make out a tax list. The result is that great numbers of those who are liable to taxes on personal property escape taxation altogether and the burden of the whole tax comes to be shifted more and more to real estate. Personal property has slipped and is slipping in ever-growing proportion from the tax lists. This is a matter of common knowledge. According to the Report of the New York State Board of Tax Commissioners, although in 1867 realty paid 74.61% of the tax on property while personalty paid 25.29% still, by 1904, real estate paid 90.64% while personalty's share had dwindled steadily to 9.36%.[1] No intelligent person would, however, doubt that in the great Empire State the value of personal property overbalances that of realty at least five or six times. In 1904 in Greater New York, realty was assessed at $4,751,-532,826 while personal property was assessed at only $680,-866,092.[2] From 1890 to 1902 the assessed value of realty in New York State increased about 57% while that of personalty increased only 43%. For the same period in New Hampshire and Vermont an actual decrease in the assessed value of personalty is shown.[2] In other words the owners of realty and the people who pay the rent are coming to bear an increasing proportion of the property tax while the owners of personalty are to a corresponding degree enabled to evade their share of the tax.

The third great criticism that must be brought against the administration of the general property tax is that some persons are doubly taxed. The best-known illustration of this tendency is in regard to mortgages. Mortgages are

[1] See report of 1904.   [2] *Ibid.*, p. 33 *et seq.*

undoubtedly valuable pieces of property and according to the strict theory of the property tax should be taxed like other property. But this leaves out of account the relations between the borrower and the lender. The lender has always the upper hand. Under threat of refusing to lend his money he may make the borrower agree to assume the tax or if he be prevented by law from such a course of procedure he can nevertheless make the borrower assume the burden by refusing to lend him the money except at a rate of interest that is high enough to reimburse him for the tax—and usually for somewhat more. Thus the borrower is taxed on what he " owes " as well as on what he "owns" while the lender goes scot-free and claims a little reward in addition. Similar, of course, is the taxation of the personal property of the individual where he is not allowed to make a deduction for his just debts, although double taxation arising from this source is, as a matter of fact, not so common because in most of the states deductions for bona-fide indebtedness can be made from the personalty assessment. In the matter of mortgages, however, there is a cruelly large amount of double taxation and this arises out of the attempt to administer the property tax according to its theoretical requirements.

The other great criticisms which must be brought against the administration of the general property tax are essentially outgrowths of the three outlined above and may, therefore, be considered secondary in origin and nature. This by no means implies, however, a secondary importance.

The first of these is that the general property tax as now administered tends to become a regressive tax—that is one whose rate increases as the amount of the base decreases. This is due to the fact, alluded to above, that personal property is slipping always in larger proportions from the tax lists and an increasingly greater proportion of the tax comes to be borne by the owners of real estate who are assessed not only on their real estate, but on their personal property as well. Of course this presses hardest on the farmer and the small landholder, almost all of whose property is listed—not because farmers and small landholders are necessarily more honest but because they could not hide their property if they wanted to. Almost everybody in the neighborhood knows how many horses, cattle, plows, wagons, etc. a farmer in any particular community has and so the farmer could hardly make a false list of these things and hope to escape detection. So it seems patent that, even though we admit that some of the farmer's property escapes, not nearly so much of it does so as is the case with the resident of a large city whose wealth is invested largely in corporate securities. Thus if I, a resident of a large city, have in reality $100,000 worth of property but succeed in having it listed, say at $25,000 (which if it is personal property is a generous assessment as things now go), whereas farmer Jones who owns in all $25,000 worth of property cannot succeed in getting his assessed at a valuation below $20,000, and if the general rate of tax is 50 cents on each $100, I pay $125 on my property while farmer Jones pays $100 on his. The actual rate I thus pay per dollar of my property is $.00125 while farmer Jones' actual rate is $.004 on his smaller holding. Thus it can hardly be gainsaid that the property tax as now administered is a regressive tax and that it bears most heavily on those who, comparatively speaking, are least able to pay.

The second criticism that may be spoken of as secondary in nature—although by no means of secondary importance either from a purely financial or from a broader social and ethical point of view—is that the general property tax as now administered puts a great premium on dishonesty and a corresponding penalty on honesty and good citizenship.

It does this in the first place because it encourages a man to list only a part of his property. Every property-holder knows that the more property he can prevent from being listed the less will be his tax. Consequently if he has some property of which he is morally sure that the assessor will not be able to trace a clue there is a great temptation for him to neglect putting such property on the list. In the second place there is a great temptation for the property holder to undervalue such property as he does list because the lower the valuation, the smaller will be the tax he will be called upon to pay. Of course the assessor is given the authority to fix the final valuation but he is at a great disadvantage as compared with the owner and he is forced in a greater or less degree to accept the owner's valuation. Real estate cannot be hid or easily undervalued but the extent to which personalty escapes taxation, as shown above, gives some idea of the extent to which the owners of personal property succumb to the temptations here referred to. In the third place the privilege generally accorded of deducting from a taxpayer's personal assessment the amount of his bona-fide indebtedness has been most unconscionably abused. Fictitious debts are easily arranged and skillful schemes of evasion—perhaps not technically illegal—have been devised. Perjury itself is not seldom resorted to. "Swearing off taxes" each fall in New York City is an annual source of newspaper wit and sarcasm. Whole assessments are sometimes wiped out because of deductions for "bona fide" indebtedness. There is thus a triple temptation for the property-holder to evade a part of his taxes. He knows that many, many others are not bearing their just share and he naturally asks himself why he should assume their burden. He knows that if he declares all of his property at its full value the tax he will have to bear will be made up not only of his just share but also of an appreciable share of others who, less scrupulous than he, listed only a part of their property. If he is honest he is thus penalized for the dishonesty of others. Thus cupidity and a natural resentment against being forced to bear the evaded responsibilities of others act as a tremendous incentive against a complete and just valuation of one's property— an incentive which only a few sterling characters can resist, and no tax against which such an indictment must be brought can be consistently justified by anybody with the modern point of view.

We have spoken of the property tax as now administered. It may be supposed that under a different scheme of administration it might work well. But here it must be said that every scheme that human ingenuity can devise has been tried—and has failed. As Professor Ely says, the more you try to improve the system of the general property tax the worse it becomes. We have long since outgrown the stage in our economic career where the tax was either equitable in principle or possible of just application. It is an anachronism which should be relegated to the limbo of the past, where it belongs.

II. *GROSS RECEIPTS AND EARNINGS TAXES:*

As a supplement of or a substitute for the general property tax on quasi-public corporations, there is employed in some of the states, a tax based on receipts and earnings. New York and Pennsylvania both have general corporation tax acts, applying to all corporations, which provide a tax on the actual value of the capital stock. The tax is somewhat progressive in nature in New York according as the dividends are above or below six per cent. At least nine other states [1] have taxes on railways based on earnings. In

[1] Delaware, Maine, Maryland, Minnesota, Mississippi, Ohio, Texas, Vermont and Virginia.

some cases the tax is an important one—as in Vermont where the tax may be in lieu of the state tax on property and franchise,—while in other cases it is only of slight significance—as in Virginia where the tax serves only to pay the expenses of the railroad commission. In the same way some of the states tax the other quasi-public corporations on the basis of earnings. In Ohio these taxes are known as excise taxes, in Mississippi and some of the other southern states they are called privilege taxes, while in still other states the tax is known simply as a " gross receipts " or a " gross earnings " tax.

Administration of the Tax: In assessing these taxes the methods employed are very similar to those employed in assessing the property tax. The company must in the first instance submit a sworn statement of the amount of its earnings and the authorities then determine the amount upon which the tax is to be levied. There is the usual apportionment of the earnings on the basis of mileage or there is at least such an apportionment of the interstate earnings a proportion of which taken together with the purely intrastate earnings is usually taken as the base of the tax. As a rule, however, the rate of the tax is fixed by law,— whether it be progressive or otherwise,—and the only duty devolving upon the authorities is the determination as to which of the prescribed rates shall apply. In all such cases also the corporations are, as a rule, given an opportunity to be heard—just as is the case in the assessment of corporate property. The certification of the taxes chargeable to each company is similarly made by the proper authorities to the companies concerned and the law also prescribes the period during which such taxes must be paid. Considering then that the differences in the methods of assessing these two kinds of taxes are no greater than they are, it is not necessary to refer to the earnings taxes with any greater particularity than has already been done.

Critical Remarks: In discussing the assessment and collection of gross-receipts taxes we are again required to call attention to the fact that we are not called upon to discuss the theory of the tax, although we do not hesitate to say that a tax on gross receipts which leaves out of account the original investment of capital and the expenses of operation is not an equitable tax in principle. But from a purely administrative point of view hardly any other tax is so easily assessed. Whatever the particular system of accounting, the gross receipts of a business must always be determined and it is thus a relatively easy matter for the state to ascertain what is its own just share. The difficulty that is presented is the determination of the proportion of the interstate earnings of the large quasi-public corporations, which should be included in the taxable gross earnings. A mileage proportion is the one that is usually applied. If this is uniformly applied by all the states concerned it is fair enough so far as the corporations paying the tax are concerned. Most of the objections that have been brought against the principle refer to an unequal distribution of advantages among the states themselves. It is contended that on a pure mileage basis of distribution of gross interstate earnings one state gets in reality more than its just share while another state or several others are correspondingly deprived of their just shares. But objections of this nature can never be entirely overcome. The ease with which a proportion of the interstate earnings can be determined on a mileage or similar basis for purposes of state taxation is a strong argument in its favor. Gross-receipts taxes are thus, as a whole, administered with great facility and this, no doubt, led the California Commission (of which Professor Carl Plehn was the Secretary) to say " taxation on gross earnings as a method for taxing railroads comes as close to perfect equity as any system that can be devised." [1]

The tax on net earnings is theoretically the ideal tax but from an administrative point of view it is much more difficult to apply than is a gross-earnings tax. Many and serious questions of capitalization and accounting are involved and these would have to be solved before the tax could be applied with anything like certain justice. The New York Corporation Tax aims somewhat in the direction of a tax on net earnings; still it represents more than such a tax alone. On the whole it may be said that we have not yet developed to the point where a net-earnings tax can be successfully administered in our states.

III. *LICENSE TAXES:*

Although liquor taxes and other license taxes are a source of very considerable revenue to the state and are of corresponding importance in the fiscal system, still the methods employed in levying such charges are relatively simple and will therefore be only cursorily dealt with here.

In the great majority of cases these "license taxes," as they are sometimes called, are certain fixed charges levied by law on specified operations—business or otherwise—or for specified privileges. In such cases the law declares illegal the exercise of a privilege for which a license is demanded, until such license charge be paid. The uniform practice is, therefore, for the person—natural or corporate—desiring such license, to apply to the proper authorities—state or local as the case may be—to show to the satisfaction of such authorities that he has fulfilled all the requirements that the law may in any particular case demand, and to pay in ac-

[1] Quoted from the *American Political Science Review*, vol. I, p. 88.

cordance with such requirements the charge that the law imposes. There is no careful process of valuation or equalization or determination of the amount to be charged. The law declares what amount is to be charged and the authorities simply withhold the license until the proper amount is paid. Penalties of sufficient stringency are provided for him who, without fulfilling the legal requirements and paying the legal fee, exercises a privilege for which a charge is prescribed and oftentimes a rather elaborate organization may be required for the proper administration of the tax—as is the case with the Excise Tax in New York—nevertheless the essential principles involved, in so far as the mere revenue aspects are concerned, are relatively simple. Therefore it would seem rather unnecessary to devote any further space in a treatise having to do simply with fiscal method, to a branch of the states' fiscal systems where the purely financial operations are, comparatively, so simple.

IV. *INHERITANCE TAXES:*

Owing to the peculiar nature of inheritance taxes and to the increasing importance to which, without doubt, they will attain, it is considered advisable to give in this place as briefly as possible an account of the methods employed in their administration. From a financial point of view they are not yet of very great importance although in Illinois for the four years 1898-1902 the return from the Inheritance Tax amounted to 7.45% of the total revenue of the state and in New York for the three years 1899-1901 the return from this source amounted to 12.01% of the state's revenue.[1] The rapid development of these taxes in the past few years points indubitably to the conclusion that their financial importance will increase materially in future years.

[1] See *Quarterly Journal of Economics*, vol. 19, p. 308.

Two writers, Mr. Solomon Huebner and Mr. H. A. Millis, have given in the Quarterly Journal of Economics [1] such a complete account of the development and the present state of the inheritance tax in our commonwealths that it would be useless to attempt to consider here anything further than those aspects with which we are particularly concerned. Neither of these writers touches upon the methods employed in assessing and collecting the tax, and as this is the phase of the situation that interests us here a little space will be devoted to it.[2]

Property Liable: The base of the Inheritance Tax is the property transferred by will, etc., to one or more beneficiaries. Just what heirs and beneficiaries are liable to taxes of this kind is determined by the laws of each state. The property which can be held liable for such taxes is only such as comes in some way under the jurisdiction of the state levying the tax, but in almost all of the twenty-six states having inheritance-tax laws, now actively in force, all the property that does come under the jurisdiction of the state is held liable to inheritance taxes. In Louisiana the theory of the law is that one which is sometimes given to justify inheritance taxes, namely, that such taxes recompense the state to some degree for the taxes on property that were evaded before the death of the devisor. This theory is consistently applied in Louisiana because the laws provide that when it can be proved to the satisfaction of the Judge of Probate that any property in question has borne its " just share of taxes " prior to the time of donation or

---

[1] Volumes 18 and 19.
[2] It may be added, however, that since the publication of Mr. Millis's article South Dakota has adopted an inheritance tax law, while that of Tennessee was declared unconstitutional by the Supreme Court of the State.

inheritance, no inheritance tax shall be charged against such property.[1] In Vermont a deduction is allowed to be made to the amount of inheritance taxes paid in other states,[2] but in the rest of the states where the tax is levied it is probable that the estate of a non-resident, situated within any particular state, would be subjected in some measure to double taxation. It is almost uniformly provided also, that a bequest to an administrator, executor, etc., in excess of what is determined by the court exercising probate jurisdiction to be a reasonable and just commission, shall be liable to the tax to the extent of such excess. In all respects, indeed, it is for the probate court to determine what part of the estate is liable to the tax and what amount each beneficiary must pay.

The *appraisement of the estate* is not, however, as a rule directly undertaken by the probate court itself. One or more competent and disinterested persons are appointed by the court to appraise the estate. The number of appraisers so appointed varies somewhat between the states. In some states only one may be appointed, in other states two, in still others three, while in still others there may be " one or more." [3] As a rule, also, appraisers are appointed for each estate or whenever the probate judge may think it necessary, but in Utah three appraisers are annually appointed in each county.[4] The appraisers proceed under the instructions of the court although in some states the law lays down certain general rules which require the appraisers to give notice to all persons interested of the time and place

---

[1] *Laws of 1904*, act 45.   [2] *Laws of 1904*, no. 20, sec. 3.

[3] In California, Colorado, New Jersey, New York, Pennsylvania, South Dakota, Wisconsin and Wyoming a single appraiser is appointed; in Minnesota two are appointed; three in Arkansas, Ohio, Utah and Washington, and "one or more" in Oregon.

[4] *Utah Laws of 1905*, ch. 119, sec. 3.

of hearing and also certain special rules governing the appraisement of real estate, etc. The appraisement when finally made is reported to the court in the form of a written statement and a duplicate of such statement must in some cases be sent to a designated state officer in order that the state's interest may be looked after.

The valuation as reported by the authorized appraiser is not necessarily final. The judge of the probate court can, as a rule, of his own motion set aside an appraisement and he may hear appeals that may be made by any interested party—including an authorized representative of the state—and the appeals may even be carried to the higher courts.[1] In Vermont the administrator or the executor, etc., may agree with the state tax commissioner concerning the valuation of an estate but such an agreement may be set aside by either the probate court or the state treasurer.[2] In all cases the aim is, of course, to deal justly with the heirs, but to see also that the state's interests are adequately protected. When the matter of the appraisement has been finally settled the court determines the amount of the taxes due.

Collection: The requirements relative to the time when such taxes are due and payable vary somewhat among the states. In Arkansas they are due and payable within one year after the death of the devisor.[3] In California they are due at the death of the devisor,[4] in Massachusetts within two years after the executor gives bond[5]—and so on. Usually, however, some provision is made that if the taxes are paid before a specified time a generous discount is allowed, while if they are not paid before the expiration of the allotted period a considerable interest charge is levied.

[1] Supreme Court of the State in Washington.
[2] *Vermont Laws of 1904,* no. 30.   [3] *Acts of 1901,* ch. clvi, sec. 4.
[4] *California Laws,* 1905, ch. cccxiv.
[5] *Laws of Massachusetts,* ch. 15, sec. 4.

The common rate of discount allowed for prompt payment is 5%. The period during which such a discount is allowed varies, however, from three months in Pennsylvania to one year in South Dakota and Wisconsin.

The rates of interest charged also vary considerably. In some states as in New York and Ohio the rate is 6%, in others—Minnesota for example—7%, in others—Oregon and Utah for example—8%, in Arkansas 9%, in New Jersey and Wisconsin 10% and in Pennsylvania 12%. In most cases it is provided that when litigation or similar unavoidable causes delay the payment of the tax a smaller rate of interest be charged—as a rule, 6%. That is to say, that in such cases no punitive charge is levied, but only such a charge as suffices to compensate the state for a real loss. In Pennsylvania it is provided that if the property does not earn as much as 6% even a smaller rate will be acceptable to the state.[1]

In nearly all cases the executor or administrator is held personally liable for the tax. If the estate be money he is authorized to deduct the amount of the tax, and if it be some other kind of property he may collect the tax from the heir. In no case is he obliged to turn over any legacy specific or otherwise to any heir until the tax is paid. Furthermore he is authorized to sell a part of the property to pay the tax—should that be necessary—just as he may be authorized by law to sell some of the property to pay the testator's debts. The primary responsibility for the payment of the tax rests, then, upon the executor or the administrator.

The tax so charged is payable either to the county or to the state authorities, although the tax is, for the most part, used for state purposes. In most cases it is to the

[1] *Laws of Pennsylvania*, col. 4489, sec. 52.

county treasurer that the tax must be paid. In Louisiana payment is made to the collector of the "Parish," in Maryland and Pennsylvania to the Register of Wills, and in a considerable number of states directly to the state treasurer.[1] Where the payment is made to the county treasurer the executor must demand duplicate receipts, one of which he must send to the proper state officer—usually the chief auditing officer—who stamps it with his seal and who attaches to it his signature. Only then is such receipt accepted by the probate court in the settlement of the executor's or the administrator's accounts. In practically the same way, when the payment is made to the state treasurer, the treasurer's receipt cannot be presented as a voucher in the settlement of the executor's accounts until it has been countersigned by the auditor. This is done in order that a proper charge may be made against the county authorities or against the state treasurer for the amounts that are due to the state. The taxes paid to the county authorities are then paid over to the state treasurer either at the regular settlement of the county treasurer with the state authorities or at a special time as the law may provide.

Enforcement of Payment: A word may be added about the enforcement of the payment of the tax in such cases where it is due and where payment has not been made. In all cases where the county treasurer or other officer believes that a tax is due and payment has not been made, he notifies the district attorney of the proper county of the facts of the case, and the district attorney upon investigation brings legal action to enforce the payment. The Judge of Probate may also cite the persons interested to appear before him and show cause why they should not be compelled to

[1] New Jersey, Ohio, North Dakota, Oregon, Utah, Vermont and Washington.

pay the taxes chargeable against them. It is also usually provided that registers of wills, judges of probate and similar officers report to the county and state authorities all estates that are liable to the tax so that no estate may evade the payment of the same. In conclusion, however, it may be said that owing to the many legal requirements concerning the administration of estates the enforcement of the inheritance-tax laws is not a matter of great difficulty.

V. OTHER SPECIAL KINDS OF TAXES:

In the preceding survey we have been unable to take into account more or less special taxes that are found in only one or a few states. Nor can we hope to do so here because of the limitations that we set out to observe. But because the State of New York—the great Empire State—has advanced farthest in its financial development and has realized more fully than any other state the ideal of the segregation of the sources of state and local revenue, a word or two will be said about two rather highly specialized taxes that characterize the fiscal system of that state. These taxes are the Stock Transfer and the Mortgage Tax.

The Stock Transfer Tax: This tax was adopted in 1905.[1] A tax of two cents is levied on each one hundred dollars of the face value of all stocks transferred—however such transfer be effected. It does not apply to the deposit of stock as collateral security, but only to stock actually sold. The tax is collected by means of the sale of adhesive stamps which must be placed to the proper amount on the certificate or other evidence of the sale of the stock. These stamps are prepared by the Comptroller and he provides for their sale. The stamps when used must be canceled by initialing, etc. In enforcing the payment of the tax the Comptroller

[1] *Laws of 1905,* ch. 241.

has power to examine the books of corporations and persons and if the tax has not been paid he may bring action in court. The maximum penalty which can be levied for failure to pay the tax is $1000 fine and six months' imprisonment. Furthermore it is provided that when the tax is not paid the transfer of stock is not legal and no action in connection therewith can be brought.[1]

The Mortgage Tax: Most states tax mortgages as they do other property but in New York the mortgage tax is simply a recording tax. As originally adopted in 1905 the tax was an annual tax of 50 cents on each $100 or major fraction thereof of the value of the mortgage but the real estate interests proved to be strong enough to have the act amended in 1906 so that as the law now stands the tax has to be paid only once.

The tax is levied on mortgages on real property in the state and such mortgages are exempt from local taxation. Payment of the tax is made to the recording officer of the county where the real estate to which the mortgage is attached, is situated. If such real estate is situated in more than one county, apportionment of the amount to be paid in each county is made by the State Board of Tax Commissioners on the basis of the relative assessed valuation of the real estate concerned. The payment of the tax is easily enforced because the recording officer simply refuses to record a mortgage until the tax is paid and no legal action of any kind can be taken in connection with a mortgage upon which the tax has not been paid.[2]

The theory of these taxes does not concern us here and they are still too new to allow any sound judgment as to

[1] This tax yielded almost 1⅓ millions in 1905 and over 6½ millions in 1906.
[2] The mortgage tax netted about half a million in 1906.

the efficiency of the administrative schemes adopted for their collection. Still no really new administrative principles are involved in either case and there seems to be no reason for expecting any serious difficulties.

Part II. Centralization of Revenue

The state's revenue collected by sundry officials scattered through the state must in some way be brought under the direct control of those officers of the state government who are charged with the responsibility of managing it. During the process of collection the funds are not under their control; they cannot spend them as the budget law directs until the money is put into their possession. This transfer of the possession of the state's revenue from the various collecting officers to the treasury officials may, of course, be accomplished in divers ways. Actual coin and bills may be sent to the state treasury or there may be simply a transfer of the right of control over certain funds by means of a bank check. However it may be done the essential nature of the transaction is the same. The control of the revenues collected must be transferred from the collecting officers to the treasury officials who must do the disbursing. This transfer of control is commonly spoken of as the centralization of revenue.[1]

The question that we are called upon to answer at this point is then as follows: What are the requirements concerning the frequency with which and the methods according to which the control of the state revenues is transferred from the collecting to the central disbursing authorities.

[1] It is hardly necessary to add that such revenue as is paid directly into the state treasury—using treasury here in the broad sense—does not need to undergo a process of centralization, and this therefore is left out of account at this place.

Considering first the question of the methods employed in transferring such control we may say that the first step requires obviously the determination of the amount of the funds to be transferred. This determination is, as a rule, based upon what is called a "settlement." That is to say that at certain times, varying according to the laws of each state and sometimes according to the source of the revenue, the collecting officer must make a statement to the central treasury official showing what funds of the state are in his possession and giving such other facts concerning them as may be required. Such a statement is, of course, always under oath. There are various ways by which a statement of this kind may be "checked" or verified but these considerations find a place in the following chapter. The point that has bearing here is that by such a settlement the amount of revenue due the state, gathered from any particular source by the officer making the settlement, is determined. The amount so determined can thereafter be transferred to the control of the state treasury officials in whole or in part as the laws of the state or the exigencies of the treasury may determine.

It was stated above that the actual transfer of the funds is accomplished in divers ways. In olden times a transfer of actual cash was made but modern methods are rather less cumbersome. Bank checks and drafts, express and postal money-orders are now the common agencies. Indeed, since in most of the states an independent treasury system has given way to the system of state and county depositories, the transfer of funds from the collecting to the disbursing officers represents very often nothing more than a transfer of credit on the books of a bank. This particular phase of the question is, therefore, not one that nowadays appears to be of much importance.

It may be wise to refer somewhat to the frequency with which these settlements are required to be made. This matter is determined by the laws of each state for the officers of such state. A large number of states—about twenty —require regular monthly settlements on the part of the local collectors or receivers of state revenue with the state treasury officials,—that is to say,—the local officers must at intervals of a month pay into the state treasury those state funds for which, according to the settlement, they are found to be liable. In South Carolina semi-monthly settlements are required [1] and in the larger cities of some of the states —Missouri, Maryland and Virginia for example—the state funds are deposited weekly. It is also found that in many states [2] the auditor and the treasurer of the state may order a settlement at any time and the local officials have to be prepared to pay over whatever state money may be in their possession. In a few states it is found that monthly payments must be made only during certain periods of the year,—those periods when the collection of the annual taxes is under way. In Indiana for example there is a regular monthly settlement on the part of the county treasurers from December to April while after April there is no regular settlement until June 15th and after that none until December 15th.[3] In Kentucky in like manner there is a regular monthly settlement only from May to December and in Florida only through November, December and January.[4] In perhaps a half-dozen states the regular and

[1] *Laws of South Carolina*, sec. 401.

[2] California, Indiana, Iowa, Montana, Nevada, Pennsylvania, South Dakota, Utah, Vermont and Wyoming.

[3] *Laws of Indiana*, sec. 5642.

[4] *Laws of Kentucky*, sec. 4143; *Laws of Florida*, title 6, ch. 1, sec. 369.

required settlements come only quarterly[1] and in others[2] only semi-annually although it must not be forgotten that in some of these states the treasury officials may order the payment of the state funds at any time. In New England, where the towns are simply called upon to pay an apportioned share of the state tax, is found only the requirement that such tax be paid before a specified date.[3] Then other states require settlements at irregular intervals or have in addition to requirements for regular settlements certain special requirements of more or less interest. In Minnesota, for example, regular settlements are provided for in February, May, and October,[4] in Utah in January, April, July, October, November and December.[5] In Idaho it is required[6] that whenever the county treasurer has $100 belonging to the state (except the state school fund) it must be paid over forthwith to the state treasurer. In Ohio the auditor may draw on the county treasurers in favor of the state at any time between December 15th and June 15th for sums not exceeding two-thirds of the current collection of taxes for state purposes and the remainder is paid over at the regular semi-annual settlements in February and August.[7] In Rhode Island all persons receiving money for the state must pay the same to the general treasurer within 30 days after receiving it.[8] In West Virginia[9] the taxes collected

[1] Arkansas, Idaho, Louisiana, Pennsylvania, South Dakota and Vermont.

[2] Kansas, Montana, Nebraska, Nevada, Oregon and Virginia.

[3] November 1st in Connecticut, for example, and September 1st in Maine.

[4] *Laws of 1897*, ch. 100. [5] *Laws of Utah*, sec. 2663.

[6] *Laws of Idaho*, sec. 1577. [7] *Laws of Ohio*, sec. 161.

[8] *Laws of Rhode Island*, title 5, ch. 20.

[9] *Laws of West Virginia*, ch. 3, sec. 25.

by the local authorities must be paid over as follows: one-half on or before June 20th in the year next after such taxes are assessed, one-fourth on or before May 1st and the remainder on or before August 1st in the same year.

It is furthermore to be noted that the revenue derived from particular sources may be specially dealt with. Without going into this phase of the situation extensively, a few examples may be of interest. In Alabama, although for the state taxes the local officers must make monthly returns, the Probate Judge is required to pay over the revenue derived from licenses, etc., only quarterly. In Colorado and Illinois and some other states where the inheritance tax is collected by the local officers it is settled for only semi-annually. In Delaware the fees received by state officers must be paid into the state treasury seven days after being received; in Massachusetts and Kentucky the revenue derived from this source is settled for monthly and in Ohio only quarterly.

Pressure of one kind or another is brought to bear on the collecting officer wherever the required settlement and payment are not promptly and properly made. In the New England states, where the idea of town responsibility is the accepted one, the property of the inhabitants of the town may be seized under an execution issued by the state treasurer, if the town's quota of state taxes is not paid within the prescribed time, although in Connecticut the estates of the selectmen are first seized.[1] The town as a whole must of course make due reparation to any inhabitant whose property has been seized and in Vermont interest as high as 12% may be claimed. As a rule it may be said that the local districts are held responsible for their share of the general state taxes. If the collecting officers abscond or default the state requires the district to pay up

[1] *Laws of Connecticut*, sec. 2378.

its quota of the taxes at a later date. In New York[1] if there are not sufficient funds in the county treasury standing to the credit of any particular town for the latter's quota of the state tax, the county treasurer is authorized to borrow money on the credit of the county, to pay such town's quota and the town must then subsequently pay the amount borrowed with interest. Penalties on the officers themselves for withholding the state's money are various. Indiana levies a penalty of 15% on the amount withheld,[2] Kentucky 6%,[3] Mississippi at a rate of 30% per annum [4] and New Jersey 10% per annum if held more than 15 days overdue.[5] In Utah the county treasurer runs the risk of losing a quarter's salary if he fails to settle when required.[6] In Wisconsin a penalty of 5% is provided and 10% interest per annum is also charged on the sums withheld and if, after a formal demand on the part of the state treasurer such payment is still refused, the penalty is increased to 10%.[7] The penalties here referred to concern for the most part the settlement by the local authorities for the property tax but penalties of a similar nature are provided in nearly all other cases as well. It would never do for the state to be lax in these matters.[8]

[1] *Laws of 1902*, ch. 378.
[2] *Laws of Indiana*, sec. 6496.
[3] *Laws of Kentucky*, sec. 4143.
[4] *Laws of Mississippi*, sec. 3840.
[5] *Laws of New Jersey*, page 3303, sec. 107.
[6] *Laws of Utah*, sec. 2664.
[7] *Laws of Wisconsin*, sec. 1117.
[8] Virginia has an almost unique provision in this particular. It is provided that (*Laws*, sec. 604 *a*):
Whereas during every session of the General Assembly it is developed that some of the county or city treasurers are in arrears to the state on account of collection of taxes, thereby depriving the Commonwealth of its just dues, which should be promptly turned into her coffers, and
Whereas, it is right and proper that the sureties of all such treas-

Thus at one time or another and in one way or another the control of the funds that are collected by officials scattered throughout the state comes finally to be centralized in the hands of the few officials upon whom rests the responsibility of distributing or disbursing the revenue according to the budget law.

Part III. Safekeeping of the Public Funds

The question of how the state should keep its public funds is one that in former days caused much more controversy than it does now. In older times not only were the stability and safety of banks seriously, and too often justly, questioned,—but the mere idea of having individuals make a gain out of the public funds was itself repugnant to the "democracy" of the period. Today better banking laws enforced with care have removed almost entirely the old distrust, while the narrow prejudice against banks as such has pretty generally been dispelled. In the national government where the independent treasury system has been in vogue since the forties various executive practices [1] have broken down somewhat the solidity of the system while in our states the independent treasury system seems to be in its last stages. One by one the state gov-

urers, as well as taxpayers, of the state should be apprised of the true facts in connection therewith; therefore

The Auditor of Public Accounts is required to have made from the books in his office annually at the end of the fiscal year a statement showing the condition of the accounts of every county or city treasurer of the Commonwealth who is in arrears to the state in his collection therefor, and a copy shall also be sent to the clerk of such city or county, who must post same at door of the court-house, etc.

It is then provided that any newspaper may copy and publish the same.

[1] These practices are based on the national bank act, which allows the Secretary of the Treasury to make deposits of money in selected banks when satisfactory collateral is pledged as security.

ernments have adopted the system of bank depositories for storing the public funds and today fully three-fourths of the states have fallen into line.

The bank depositories employed are national and state banks and, in a few states, also trust companies. Besides her own banks and trust companies New Hampshire allows those of Massachusetts to be depositories of the state funds.[1] This is a rather unique provision, however, and the general rule is to limit the privilege of acting in this capacity in each state to the national banks doing business in such state and to state banks and trust companies organized under the law of the same.

The choice of the particular institutions to be employed in any state is, of course, one of considerable importance. The most important factor in this choice is that of security while the second is that of comparative advantage to the state in the employment of one institution rather than another. A few of the states [2] require a bank to have a prescribed amount of paid-up capital before it can be chosen as a depository, but in the others it is recognized that there are other ways of guaranteeing the security of the funds, and preliminary requirements of this kind are not insisted upon.

Method of Choice: The methods employed in choosing the state depositories it may be said that different officers are responsible in different states. In some states [3] the treasurer alone is responsible. In other states the treasurer may not act alone but requires the approval of other of the state officials. In some four states, for example,[4] the treas-

[1] *Laws of 1905,* ch. 68.

[2] Kentucky $100,000, West Virginia $20,000, Rhode Island $500,000.

[3] Kentucky, Minnesota, Nebraska, South Dakota and Texas, for example.

[4] California, Florida, South Carolina and Virginia.

urer proceeds only with the advice and consent of the governor and the auditor. In Georgia and Maryland the governor and in Tennessee and New York the comptroller alone need to be consulted. In Iowa the Executive Council and in Massachusetts and New Hampshire the governor and his council form the advisory board. Then it is found that still other states vest the entire responsibility in special boards. In Kansas, for example, the Board of Treasury Examiners composed of the Governor, Secretary of State and State Auditor is a special board for the purpose.[1] In North Dakota the responsibility referred to is vested in the Board of Auditors which acts with the Governor,[2] and in West Virginia in the Board of Public Works.[3] Ohio and Wisconsin have each a special " Board of Deposit " composed of the Treasurer, Auditor and Attorney General in Ohio, and the Commissioners of Public Lands and the Governor in Wisconsin.[4]

The principles employed in determining the selection may or may not be prescribed by law. In some states—Connecticut and New Jersey for instance—full discretion is allowed to the responsible officers. In other states the laws make only general suggestions. In New Hampshire, for example, it is provided that " other things being equal " the preference shall be given to those banks which allow interest on daily balances,[5] in Florida the choice must be made according to the " best inducements " offered [6] and in New

[1] State Deposit Act of 1905.
[2] *Laws of North Dakota*, sec. 237.
[3] *Laws of West Virginia*, ch. 17.
[4] Bates, *Laws of Ohio* (1787-1906, pp. 200-3) ; *Laws of Wisconsin*, sec. 160.
[5] *Session Laws of New Hampshire*, 1905, ch. 68.
[6] *Laws of 1897*, ch. 4586.

York[1] and Rhode Island[2] according to the highest rate of interest allowed—and so on. In still other states definite modes of procedure are prescribed, bids must be received and formally opened and the choice must be made according to the terms thereof.[3] The nature and contents of these bids naturally vary from state to state. A bid may have to do only with the rate of interest that the bank will pay—as in California—or it may have to do also with the amount of funds that such bank may desire. In Ohio banks desiring to be designated as state depositories must file applications before the meeting of the Board of Deposit and must append to such applications sworn statements of their financial condition.[4] In Kansas and Texas each bank must deposit with its bid a certified check for $250 and $500 respectively, which is forfeited if the bank should fail to comply with its bid or proposal in the event that it is chosen as one of the depositories.[5] Moreover in some of the states a minimum rate of interest is prescribed;[6] 2% is the common minimum rate although in Wisconsin it is 2½%. As a rule, however, no minimum rate is prescribed because it is recognized that conditions might arise where the minimum rate would be unobtainable and it would be inadvisable to tie the treasurer's hands in such cases. A few of the states which prescribe a minimum rate obviate the difficulty here suggested by allowing the treasurer to make special deposits for safekeeping at any

[1] *New York Finance Law*, art. 1, sec. 8.
[2] *Laws of Rhode Island*, title vi, ch. 33.
[3] California, Kansas, Missouri, North Dakota and Texas.
[4] Bates, *Laws of Ohio*, 1787-1906, pp. 200-4.
[5] Kansas: State Depository Act, 1905; and Texas: *Laws of 1905*, ch. 164.
[6] Bates, *Laws of Ohio*, 1787-1906, pp. 200-4.

time, but in such cases a prescribed minimum rate of interest serves but little purpose beyond suggesting what may be considered a fair rate. The interest so received is ordinarily calculated on the basis of daily average balances.[1] The various points hereinbefore referred to indicate then the general requirements or principles according to which the choice of the depositories is made.

The number of depositories that may be chosen also differs from state to state. In Delaware the Farmer's Bank in which the state is interested is practically the sole depository. Massachusetts on the other hand has a very large number. In Georgia a depository is chosen in each of 43 cities that are designated by law.[2] In Iowa " one or more " is chosen in Des Moines. In New York the depositories are restricted to the cities of New York and Albany but the number is left to the discretion of the treasurer and the comptroller.[3] In Kansas the number may not be less than ten and in Kentucky not less than three nor more than five. In most cases, however, the responsible officials are given considerable discretion in this particular.

A few of the states lay down also certain rules which are aimed to prevent discrimination in favor of any particular bank or banks in the deposit of public funds. In California for example, according to the constitutional amendment which was responsible for the depository act of 1905, no officer may deposit more than 20% of public funds available at one time for deposit in any bank when there are

[1] As a matter of fact the rate commonly obtained varies slightly about 2% to 3%. The amount of revenue obtained from this source approximates at present $120,000 to $140,000 annually in New York, $120,000 in Massachusetts, $50,000 to $60,000 in New Jersey, and $30,000 to $40,000 in Ohio.

[2] *Laws of Georgia*, sec. 982.

[3] *Finance Law*, art. 1, sec. 8.

other qualified banks requesting such deposits. The law of 1905 goes even further and permits only one-tenth of the available amount of state money to be placed in any one depository. In Kansas the law directs the treasurer to make his deposits in "proportionate amounts" and to draw his checks on the several depositories in the same way.[1] In Missouri the funds of the state are divided into twenty equal parts and the banks bid for the amounts they desire.[2] In Texas the treasurer is directed to maintain as nearly as possible an equal balance in each bank in proportion to the amount each is entitled to receive.[3] That rules of this kind are often necessary is shown by the revelations arising out of the wrecking of the Enterprise bank in Pennsylvania hardly a year ago.

The security of the funds placed with depositories is safeguarded in a number of states by certain special provisions.

In the first place it is found that at least ten of the states require the depositories to give bond. In some cases the amount of this bond is specified, being $25,000 in Texas and $50,000 in Georgia, Virginia and West Virginia. In Kentucky the minimum amount of the bond alone is prescribed ($100,000). In Minnesota and Montana the amount of the bond must be at least double the amount of the deposits while in Nebraska, North Dakota and Wisconsin the amount must be approved by the proper authorities.

A second method related somewhat to the first requires the depositories to deposit with the state adequate security for such funds as may be entrusted with them. At least ten[4] of the states employ this method, among them being

---

[1] Depository Act, 1905.   [2] *Laws of Missouri*, sec. 10453.
[3] *Texas Law of 1905*, ch. 164.
[4] California, Florida, Kansas, Maryland, Michigan, Missouri, North Carolina, Ohio, South Dakota and Texas.

Texas which was mentioned as one of the states requiring a bond from depositories. The amount of security so required depends, as a rule, upon the amount of funds deposited with any particular bank. In Texas the amount is fixed—$50,000 in U. S. bonds, Texas bonds or those of the minor divisions of the state.[1] In South Dakota the amount is $250,000 and never less than the deposit.[2] In California the amount must be at least 10% in excess of deposits[3] while in Kansas and Ohio the deposits need merely to be covered.[4] In the other states the security must be simply " ample " or " sufficient."

The third and last method of guaranteeing the security of deposited funds has to do with the limitations on the amounts that may be deposited. In some cases this limitation is expressed in terms of percentages of the capital stock, in other cases in fixed amounts and in still others in terms of a percentage of the bond given or security deposited. In California, for example, the constitution prohibits deposits in a bank above 50% of the bank's capital and the state law goes a step further and makes the maximum 25% of such capital. Tennessee also limits the state's deposits in any bank to one-fourth of the bank's capital.[5] In Connecticut the state's funds in a bank may not exceed 30% of the bank's capital, surplus and undivided profits.[6] Nebraska places a similar maximum at 30% of the capital,[7] Massachusetts and New Hampshire at 40% and Kansas at 75%.[8] In

[1] *Laws of 1905*, ch. 164. [2] *South Dakota Laws*, sec. 341.
[3] *Laws of 1905* (California), ch. cccviii.
[4] Kansas State Depository Act, 1905; and Ohio, *Bates Laws*, 1787-1906, pp. 200-6.
[5] *Laws of Tennessee*, sec. 281. [6] *Laws of Connecticut*, sec. 1969.
[7] *Laws of Nebraska*, sec. 5088.
[8] Massachusetts: *Laws*, ch. 6, sec. 61; New Hampshire: *Laws of 1905*, ch. 68; and Kansas: *Depository Act of 1905*.

North Dakota the maximum is the "assessed value" of "paid up capital"[1] and simply the "paid up capital" in Ohio and Wisconsin.[2] Kansas also limits the deposits of the state in any bank to $100,000;[3] Maine to $20,000, except in the bank through which the treasurer may wish to meet the interest on the state debt;[4] Texas to $50,000 and Ohio to $500,000.[5] Then, finally, in Nebraska the deposits of the state in any depository may not exceed 50% of the bond of such depository,[6] and in West Virginia three-fourths of such bond.[7] Wisconsin allows a deposit up to the amount of the bond[8] and Georgia allows the deposits to exceed the bond but not for a period longer than ten days.[9]

It must, however, be also observed that some of the states do not regard it as necessary to safeguard their funds in banks, with special requirements that do not apply equally to the deposits of private individuals.

Critical Remarks: On the whole the system of state depositories has worked well. Petty scandals have of course arisen in a few states. In Pennsylvania indeed the democrats of Philadelphia were moved to insert the following in the platform of 1905: " The same corrupt ringsters who have plundered Philadelphia dominate and mis-

[1] *Laws of North Dakota,* sec. 237.

[2] Ohio: *Bates Laws,* 1787-1906, pp. 200-5; and *Wisconsin Laws,* sec. 160.

[3] Kansas, *supra cit.*

[4] *Laws of Maine,* ch. 2, sec. 58.

[5] Bates, *Ohio Laws,* 1787-1906, pp. 200-5; and Texas, *Laws of 1905,* ch. 164.

[6] *Laws of Nebraska,* sec. 5088.

[7] *Laws of West Virginia,* ch. 17.

[8] *Laws of Wisconsin,* sec. 160.

[9] *Laws of Georgia,* sec. 989.

govern the state. The citadel of their power is the office of state treasurer. By distributing state funds among favored banks they insidiously bribe eminent respectables who otherwise would not close their eyes to rascality." And in Ohio, too, a legislative investigation into the affairs of Hamilton County showed how the interest paid by the banks was systematically appropriated by the "ring" treasurer. But these evils have been comparatively few and they are of the kind that stricter legal provisions can be expected to eradicate. There is hardly any question that in time all the state governments and probably also the national government [1] will come to adopt the system of using banking institutions as depositories for the public funds because it is the system that the consensus of the best opinion supports.

Part IV. Disbursement

In the first chapter of this treatise reference was made to the fact that the basic principle of modern constitutionalism is that of the popular control of the public purse. Payments can be made from the public treasury only in pursuance of an appropriation made by law and such law must, of course, emanate from the representatives of the people. This theory is fundamental to our American institutions and is universally applied in all our governmental organizations.

The strict prohibition placed upon the executive officers of the government against the expenditure of the public funds for any purpose not fully authorized by law makes it

---

[1] It is interesting to note that one of the recommendations of the New York Chamber of Commerce just made (November, 1906) in connection with the reform of our currency involves the abandonment of the independent treasury system.

necessary for some one to determine just what expenditures are authorized. There has grown up in consequence, in all constitutional governments, one set of officials whose chief duty it is to study and interpret the law authorizing the expenditure of the public funds and who determine the authenticity of claims presented in accordance with such laws and the identity of the persons to whom payments may be justly due, and another set of officials who have immediate charge of the state's funds and who actually pay the bills of the state when authorized by the officials of the first class. Stourm speaks of these two kinds of officials as "ordinators"[1] and "payers" ("ordonnateurs" and "payeurs"). The "ordinators" authorize the payment of the various bills of the state when they are satisfied that such payments are fully covered by lawful appropriations and the "payers" actually deliver the money for such bills to the persons entitled to receive it, when the orders to pay them are duly presented.

The great diversity of the activities of and the huge sums expended by the great national governments have of necessity given rise to a more or less complicated organization of the "ordinators" and the "payers;" but in our states, where the governmental activity is not so diversified and the sums expended are relatively small the organization here referred to is simple. Not stopping to point out minor differences it may be said that the financial departments of our various states are divided into two parts—one the office of the "Auditor" or the "Comptroller" and the other the office of the "Treasurer." The auditor or comptroller

[1] It is difficult to supply an English equivalent for "ordonnateur." The word "orderer," besides sounding very awkward, conveys an idea of too much authority. The "ordinator" really has not final authority in ordaining that a payment be made. The payer has the right to refuse an illegal payment.

is the bookkeeper of the state and is, as a rule, in general charge of the state's finances. He may and usually does have one or more deputies whose duties for the most part he prescribes and besides these he has, of course, the necessary office force. He is also the officer who in almost all of our states authorizes the payments out of the state treasury although in a few of the states [1] the chief responsibility in this particular is vested in the governor. The state treasurer on the other hand is the keeper of the public moneys. His chief responsibility is to see that the funds are safely kept. He too has, as a rule, one or more deputies and a sufficient office force. He is the officer who on the "order" of the auditor or comptroller or governor, as the case may be, pays out the money to liquidate the state's various obligations. It must not be supposed that he exercises absolutely no authority over such payments. He himself must be satisfied that the "order" or "warrant" from the auditor has been issued in accordance with the law and he has the right to refuse payment on "warrants" that are not legally issued. At best, however, he has only a veto on such warrants. He can make no payments without the "warrant" or "order" unless there are specific legal requirements to the contrary.[2] In general, then, it may be said that the auditor's department in our states has to do with the "ordering" or the "authorizing" of the payments out of the public treasury while the treasurer's de-

[1] Georgia, Maine, Massachusetts and New Hampshire.

[2] There are certain payments for which the treasurer needs no warrant from the auditing department. These are payments to the members of the two houses of the legislature, which are made on the order of the presiding officer of each for salaries of the members, etc., and the payments of the interest on the state bonds or the principal when due. The coupons of the bonds, or the bonds themselves when finally surrendered, are sufficient vouchers for the treasurer.

partment is concerned with the duty of actually paying out the amounts pursuant to such orders.

Payments out of the state treasury are made on "warrants" or "orders" issued by the auditor or comptroller. In a few cases these warrants, as has been said, are issued by the governor but even in such cases the preliminary examination is made by the state's auditing department. More will be said about this examination in the following chapter. It will suffice here to say that when satisfied as to the lawfulness of any particular claim for money from the state the auditor makes out his warrant directing the treasurer to pay the amount determined to be due to the person entitled to receive the same. Before these warrants become valid, however, they must in most states be countersigned by the state treasurer, in Florida by the Governor and in Georgia where they are originally issued under the authority of the Governor they must be countersigned by the Comptroller. It is, as a rule, the auditor's business to see to it that the warrants are so countersigned and before issuing any warrant he must, in all cases, enter in a proper book a full record of the same.

The treasurer too must keep in his office a full record of each warrant presented to him—the name of the payer, the date, on what account paid and out of what fund, according to what appropriation issued, etc. When the various requirements of this kind have been fulfilled the treasurer pays over the cash to or makes out his check on one of the depositories in favor of the person entitled to receive the same, or, in case the warrant has been turned in, in payment of some obligation due the state he gives a proper receipt for the amount of the warrant and the warrant is then canceled.

Thus the funds of the state are again finally distributed. There is first the collection of the revenue and the gradual increase in the amount of the funds in the treasury. Then follows the disbursement according to the lawful appropriations and a consequent diminution of the state's funds. It is like the flow and ebb of the tides. The whole process we have considered as the "Execution of the Budget" and now, after a wearisome chapter, having come to the end of that process, there remain to be considered in the final chapter certain points which have to do with the ultimate determination as to whether the budget law was properly executed or not. For want of a better name this chapter has been designated the "Control of the Budget."

CHAPTER V

THE CONTROL OF THE BUDGET

THE budget law in its entirety provides for the collection of certain funds for the state and also for the application of such funds after collection has been made. The "control of the budget" would then have to do with the means employed for ensuring the honest execution of the budget law in accordance with its provisions. This implies on the one hand the question of efficient administration and on the other the vital constitutional question of the ultimate control of the public purse.

On the side of collection there are no particular problems that present themselves except those that have to do with the enforcement of honesty on the part of the agents of the state in collecting and turning over the revenue due the state and those that have to do with questions of justice to the various taxpayers. Sufficient reference has already been made to these particular points in the general discussion relating to the execution of the budget.

On the side of expenditure, however, serious constitutional principles are involved. There is not only the necessity of enforcing common honesty on the part of the officials of the state in the handling of the funds that are entrusted to them but also the necessity of guaranteeing that such funds shall be applied in accordance with the will of the representatives of the people as expressed in the budget law. If the law directs that the public money be applied in specified ways while the officers of the state without fear of being discovered or called to account apply such money for purposes not sanctioned by the law the popular control of the purse would in effect be nothing more than a shadowy theory. It is here then, on the side of disbursement, that the question of the control of the budget has its greatest importance.

In discussing the question of disbursements in the last chapter it was necessary to refer to two classes of officers who are chiefly concerned with the distribution of the public funds. Following Stourm's designation these were referred to as the " ordinators " and the " payers " and it is here that a further word or two must be said about them.

The function of the " ordinators," as was stated in the chapter referred to, is to determine whether any particular expenditure is fully in accordance with the will of the representatives of the people as expressed in the budget law or acts of appropriation and if that proves to be the case, to authorize the " payers " to turn over to the one entitled to receive the same, the amount that may be declared due. This constitutes in essence a judicial function since it has to do with interpreting and declaring the meaning of a law as well as defining its application. Although this is thus essentially a judicial function it is not one that is entrusted to the regular courts, but in all constitutional governments it is vested in a special administrative office or bureau whose responsibility to the people or their representatives can thus be made much more direct.

A complication is, however, introduced by the fact that our popular representative assemblies are made up of groups of members of different political faiths and between such groups rivalry, more or less intense, always exists. One group is in control at one time and another at another, according to the changes in popular sentiment. These changes of control or changes of "administration" as we call them, would necessarily react upon the "ordinators" here being discussed, if their own official positions were in any manner affected by them. They might be disposed to sanction what would be in reality an illegal expenditure simply out of sympathy for or fear of the administration. Consequently the effort has been made in most constitutional governments to remove the "authorizing" or "ordaining" authority as far as possible from the influence of politics and to render it as independent as the general form of government will permit. In England, for example, the Audit Department at the head of which is the Auditor and Controller General, is a branch of the permanent civil service. The Auditor and Controller General is independent of the "government" because he is an appointee of the Crown and because he holds his office despite cabinet changes. Yet he is held thoroughly responsible to Parliament representing the people as a whole. There is a committee of the House of Commons which regularly "audits the Audit Department." This committee according to Woodrow Wilson [1] is made up of the most experienced business men in the Commons and before it all the accounts of the completed financial year are passed in review.

In the general government of the United States the Comptroller of the Treasury and his Auditors perform the services of examination before a warrant is issued on any account although as a matter of fact warrants are issued in the name and must bear the signature of the Secretary of the Treasury. The general independence of the Comptroller's department is guaranteed by the independence of the Treasury Department itself which is placed in a position of authority in all matters relating to the government

[1] *Congressional Government*, p. 144.

accounts. Direct and regular popular investigation into the affairs of the Comptroller's department, such as characterizes the practice of the British Parliament in relation to the Audit Office, is, however, wanting. In 1814 Congress provided for a congressional auditing committee to go over the various accounts of the Treasury Department but such regular investigation is no longer carried on.[1] The abstract constitutional principle of the popular control of the public purse would seem to demand such a final investigation by the representatives of the people; but questions of expediency, traditional practice and the ever-present possibility of examination and calling to account may materially modify the application of the principle and make regular examinations unnecessary. Congress has, of course, the right to make at any time a special examination of the Treasury Department and every other department and the growth of reprehensible practices is thus effectually checked.

In considering now more particularly the control of the budget in our states we shall take up first the payment of money from the treasury or the examination of the claims and bills that are to be liquidated by such payments, and in the second place a few words will be said concerning the examination of the accounts and records of the officers of the state who are concerned in the handling of the public revenues.

The auditing of the bills or claims which call for payment from the treasury is in most of the states entrusted to the auditor's or comptroller's department. The auditor or the comptroller who is the responsible head of such department is in most of the states elected by the people, although in a few states he holds his office by virtue of appointment on the part of the governor or the legislature.

---

[1] H. C. Adams, *Science of Finance*, p. 200.

In some states[1] however, bills or claims are audited by special boards known variously as the Board of Examiners, the Board of Auditors and the State Auditing Board. These boards are made up of some of the executive officers of the state according to the laws of the particular state concerned. It deserves mention also that in some states there are special boards for the auditing of all claims against certain special funds. In California and Nevada for instance there is a special Board of Military Auditors which audits all claims against the military fund.

It may be said at this point that in auditing any claim against the state the object is to establish the validity of the claim under the laws. In all the states a distinction is made between those claims which are covered by appropriations and those which are not so covered but which have, nevertheless, a legitimate right to be recognized. For the latter claims it is customary to give a certificate for the amount found to be due but no payment of money is made until the whole matter has been reported to the legislature. Any other procedure would as a rule be unconstitutional. In regard to claims or bills that are fully covered by appropriations the duty of the auditing authority is to determine the validity of every claim presented, to establish the right of the person claiming the money to such amount and, when satisfied as to both the validity of the claim and the identity of the claimant, to see to it that the necessary " order " or warrant is issued.

The general nature of such examination and determination may be shown by the requirements in New York. In this state the comptroller may not draw his warrant for claims except salaries and similar expenditures the amounts of which are definitely and specifically fixed by law, unless

[1] California, Idaho, Maine, Michigan, Montana, Nevada, North Dakota and Utah.

the person presenting the same presents a detailed statement of items and makes all reports required of him by law. If such a statement is for services rendered or articles furnished it must show when, where, to whom and under what authority they were rendered or furnished. If it is for traveling expenses it must show the distance traveled and between what places as well as the duty or business for the performance of which the expenses were incurred and the dates and the items of each. If the statement is for transportation, furniture or supplies, etc., a bill duly receipted must be attached to the same and finally, every such statement must bear the claimant's oath to the effect that it is just and correct. It may be added also that the auditing authorities in the states are vested with the power of summoning witnesses and examining books and with such other powers as are necessary to enable such authorities to get at all the facts that may throw light upon the general validity of the claim.

An appeal from the decision of the auditing authority is always provided for. In most cases when the claimant is dissatisfied with the decision rendered it is required that the matter be reported as soon as possible with all the evidence, etc., to the legislature and the legislature then deals with the matter as it sees fit. Some legislative committee, usually a "Committee on Claims," takes the whole question in charge and whatever action is taken by the legislature rests, as a rule, upon the report of such committee. But in Nebraska and West Virginia an appeal to the courts may be taken. In West Virginia any person having a claim against the state which the auditor has disallowed may apply by petition to the circuit court of the county in which the seat of government is to have the claim audited and adjusted.[1] In Nebraska the appeal is

---

[1] *Laws of West Virginia*, ch. 37, sec. 1.

taken to the district court and may be carried to the supreme court of the state.[1] The practice of giving the courts either an original or appellant jurisdiction in matters relating to the expenditure of public money is, however, on the whole, very uncommon.

In general the problem that underlies the question of the control of the budget is on the one hand to keep the auditing authority sufficiently independent to remove it from the influences of politics and on the other hand to prevent it from becoming too arbitrary. An auditing board composed of selected state officers is too strongly under the influence of the administration and might easily connive at a departure from the provisions of the law. Furthermore, where the auditing authority is vested in a single officer and his department, even though such officer and department do enjoy in the matter of the state accounts a considerable independence, still the fact remains that the term of office of the auditor or comptroller is in most cases subject to the uncertainties of politics and his independence from political influences is thus of necessity a doubtful and a precarious one. From the point of view of independence then it cannot be said that the general system of auditing claims and allowances in our states compares very favorably with the English system. How badly our system can be made to work at times is shown by the recent exposures in Pennsylvania by Treasurer Berry. Enormous outlays were made ostensibly for parquette floors in the new capitol that should not have cost half the amount charged. A careful and honest auditing of the various bills presented would have prevented this diversion or squandering of the people's money.

There is of course not the slightest danger of the growth of arbitrary power in the hands of the audit-

[1] *Laws of Nebraska*, sec. 5055.

ing authorities in the states. The general provision for an appeal to the legislature in cases of unsatisfactory decisions on claims is one safeguard — and a mighty one. Furthermore at least nine states [1] have provisions for the regular examination of the auditor's office on the part of the legislature, and in all of the states there hangs over the head of every department in the state government the possibility of a special legislative investigation at any time. Again, in addition to the reports that are regularly required, special reports covering any particular field may be required at any time. Thus whether there is a regular legislative investigation or not there is no danger that the legislature will lose control of the situation. The control of the purse by the representatives of the people is a principle too firmly imbedded in our institutions to permit executive or administrative aggression in this respect at the expense of the legislative authority.

Heretofore we have been concerned mostly with the auditing of claims—as they are technically called—or payments that are made originally out of the state treasury. There is, however, a further question of control which has to do with the auditing of the general accounts in the offices of the state government and of the institutions supported by the state. This is largely a question of enforcing honesty in the handling of the public funds, but it implies also a testing of the sundry expenditures made by such offices and institutions in order to ascertain whether they have been made conformably to law. But these two phases of the question go hand in hand and no attempt will be made to distinguish between them.

The auditor's or comptroller's department has in all of

[1] Arkansas, Colorado, Delaware, Florida, Georgia, Louisiana, Missouri, North Dakota and Vermont.

the states more or less full control of all matters relating to accounts and the system of accounting to be employed, and the tendency is strongly marked to give the department power to enforce a uniform system of accounting among all the offices of the state, the state institutions and the counties. Indeed it is in the matter of accounts that the state's direct supervision of the county government is more marked than in any other particular. The accounts of the county auditors and treasurers throughout the states are regularly audited at least once a year by the state authorities. The time for such inspection is not fixed but without previous notice the auditor or the comptroller himself or a deputy or special examiner bears down upon the county officers and makes an examination of the books and records of their offices. Full reports must as a rule be made to the governor or to the legislature and discrepancies should therefore be easy to detect. For the various state institutions the examination of the accounts is about the same. There has been a very encouraging improvement throughout the country concerning the accounting in these institutions. Some states have special accountants whose chief business it is to look after the accounting in the institutions of the state. The Fiscal Supervisor of Charities in New York and the Public Examiner in Minnesota are cases in point. Special legislative committees of investigation are also common. We cannot go into details here concerning the auditing of accounts in the counties and the institutions supported wholly or in part by the state but suffice it to say that in practically all of the states the attempt either has been or is being made to obtain a greater uniformity in the systems of accounting among the counties and the state institutions and a more careful inspection and examination of such accounts is thus becoming always more easily possible.

The accounts of the state treasurer, by whom all the money of the state is in the first instance paid out, are in every state required to be periodically and thoroughly audited.[1] There are in the first place many requirements as to the examination of such accounts by the auditor or comptroller. In some states [2] the accounts of the state treasurer must be examined by the auditor or comptroller once a year; in a large number of others the examination must be quarterly and in still others [3] monthly. In Ohio there is a weekly comparison of accounts and at the regular quarterly settlement of the treasurer's accounts the governor may require the secretary of state or the attorney general to be present and the officer so chosen must endorse the certificates of the settlement with his signature.[4] In Kentucky a certificate of the monthly settlement must each month be filed with the secretary of state, and he reports the same to the General Assembly during the first ten days of each session.[5] In some of the states,[6] moreover, the treasurer must make a daily statement to the auditor of the business of each day. Special provisions concerning the surrender of redeemed warrants, coupons of bonds, etc., are also common. In Florida the treasurer must submit a trial balance sheet each month to the governor while in New Jersey the treasurer must file annually a similar sheet signed by the Auditing Committee. Thus almost every state has some special provision of its own in this particular. Moreover in al-

[1] Similar requirements cover the accounts in every other state office where there are financial transactions. We shall confine ourself here, however, to the purely fiscal officers.
[2] Massachusetts and Pennsylvania, for example.
[3] Idaho and Maryland, for example.
[4] *Laws of Ohio*, sec. 192.
[5] *Laws of Kentucky*, sec. 159.
[6] California and Minnesota.

most all of the states there is an express provision in the law which enables the auditor or comptroller to examine the books and accounts of the treasurer whenever he sees fit.

In the next place there are in at least half of the states special boards or officers who are charged with the duty of examining the treasurer's books. In nine of the states [1] there is a regular auditing board or board of examiners who must examine the treasurer's books and accounts either annually or a prescribed minimum number of times each year, although in some cases the board may exercise its own discretion in the matter. These boards are made up of a few of the state executive officers as the governor, secretary of state and auditor in Kansas, or the governor, secretary of state and attorney general in Minnesota, or the secretary of state, auditor and attorney general in North Dakota. In Indiana and Ohio whenever the public interest requires it the governor appoints an expert accountant who acts with the secretary of state in the examination. In other states there is express provision for the regular or occasional appointment of a special examining officer who besides other examinations must conduct one into the accounts of the treasurer. In some states such as Idaho and Wyoming he is given the title of Special Examiner, in Vermont that of Inspector of Finance while in other states he enjoys no such title or official designation. In all cases the office is filled by appointment by the governor and the reports of the examination have to be made to him. The governor himself is often required to examine the accounts of the treasurer and the state of the treasury. In Georgia and Maryland for example the state constitutions require the governor to examine the treasurer under oath,—quarterly

[1] California, Connecticut, Kansas, Michigan, Minnesota, Montana, Nevada, New Hampshire and Utah.

in Georgia and semi-annually in Maryland. In Iowa the governor must himself at least four times a year examine the treasurer or he must appoint a committee for the purpose[1]. Finally, Kansas and North Dakota, which have special boards of examiners whose duty it is among other things to audit the accounts of the treasurer, have provisions also for special officers in addition to such boards. In North Dakota such officer is regularly appointed but in Kansas he is appointed only when the governor deems it necessary.

Thus it would seem that so far as the law can go a wide and sufficient administrative examination is provided for the state treasurer's office. But the efficiency of such examination cannot always be guaranteed. There is reason to believe from happenings in some of the states that in some cases at least the examinations are perfunctory and that political influences are sometimes brought to bear to prevent them from being thorough or searching. Much depends upon the character of the responsible officials concerned, because the provisions of law in all these cases are necessarily very general and where this is true the ultimate responsibility is on the voters themselves for they elect the officials.

In addition to the administrative examination of the accounts of the treasurer there is always a more or less thorough legislative examination. In all the states the treasurer must make a report to the legislature either directly or through the governor. These reports cover all the operations of the treasury in detail for the fiscal period. But in addition to these regular reports there is in a considerable number of states direct investigation into the affairs of the treasurer's office by a special legislative committee. At

[1] *Laws of Iowa*, sec. 184.

least eleven of the states have explicit statutory provisions concerning the appointment of such committees and in all of the states a legislative investigation may be provided for at any time. The committees are authorized, as a rule, to employ expert accountants, etc., and are given whatever other powers are necessary to enable them to conduct a thorough examination. Special reports may also be called for at any time, but these are less common in the states than in the national government. The power of the legislative branch of the government to examine thus into the affairs of all the civil officers of the state with whatever degree of thoroughness may suit its convenience is an integral part of our institutions and although this power may not be always or regularly used the possibility of its employment hangs like a warning sword over every official's head.

Concerning the examinations into the accounts of the auditing department some references have already been made in relation to the auditing of claims and bills payable out of the state treasury. Referring at this point more broadly to the accounts in general it may be said that this department also is subject, in a greater or less degree, to administrative examination. The control of the accounts of the various other officers of the state by the auditing department renders it impossible that any of the other ordinary administrative officers should be vested with the authority to examine the accounts of such department. In all of the states, however, the governor as chief executive officer enjoys the power of requiring information from the officers of the state or of examining into the affairs of their offices whenever he sees fit. In Georgia and Maryland the governor is required to examine the comptroller under oath as well as the treasurer. The constitution of Kentucky requires the General Assembly to provide by law for a monthly examination into the accounts of the auditor and the results of these examinations must be regularly reported to the governor.[1] Furthermore a considerable number of states provide for the examination of the accounts of the auditing department by the special officers and boards that were spoken of in connection with the examination of the treasurer's accounts. As was indicated in the case of the treasurer, so here, these examinations may be prescribed for specified periods of time or a minimum number may be prescribed for each year or the matter may be left entirely to the discretion of the boards or officers themselves or to that of the governor.

It may be said also that in at least a third of the states there are special provisions for legislative investigation into the affairs of the department here being discussed. Standing or special committees of examination are provided for either by constitutional or statutory enactment or by the rules of the legislature itself. The committees are for the most part the same ones that are required to audit the accounts of the treasury department and they are thus enabled to check the accounts of one department by those of the other. Furthermore regular reports covering the entire transactions of the fiscal period must be made to the legislature at each session. Here also it deserves to be mentioned that, irrespective of what the regular requirements may be, there is not the slightest doubt about the power of the legislature to provide for any examination it may deem appropriate into the affairs and records of the auditor's or comptroller's department.

Although there is thus in the various phases of the control of the budget a large measure of administrative and legislative examination and control there is little or no control on the part of the regular judiciary so far as the state

[1] Sec. 53.

officers are concerned. Grand jury investigations into the affairs of county and municipal officers are, however, quite common. The constitution of Colorado does indeed provide that the District Court of the county, wherein the seat of government is, may appoint committees of the grand jury or other persons not exceeding five to investigate the affairs in the offices of the state treasurer and state auditor.[1] Furthermore it goes without saying that in any action brought to remove any officer for discrepancies discovered or for recovery on his bond the court reviews all the evidence that is submitted and thus really decides whether or not a discrepancy exists. On the whole, though, the fact remains that the jurisdiction of the courts in these matters is only secondary in character. In practice the administrative examination is the most important, although theoretically chief importance attaches to that of the legislature.

Here at the end, however, it must be said that one of the greatest factors in the control of the budget in our country is publicity. The final authority is after all the people as a whole and public opinion is the ultimate tribunal. Reference has already been made to the fact that reports of receipts and expenditures of the state must be published at regular intervals, but in addition to this well-recognized constitutional requirement every state demands a much wider publicity of the acts of its officers. In every jurisdiction enjoying any degree of independence in financial matters—however small and insignificant such jurisdiction may be—it is required of the officers in charge that they report in some way to the people. The reports may have to be simply written reports that are posted in public places or they may be even a little more important and may have to be published in a newspaper circulating in such jurisdic-

---

[1] *Constitution of Colorado,* art. xii, sec. 5.

tion; but if the office concerned is one of broader and more general importance, the reports have, as a rule, to be printed in book or pamphlet form so that every interested citizen may examine them carefully in his home. The theory here is that the people have the right—and indeed it is considered their duty—to know how their business is being carried on. In Washington the general public has the authority to go right into the treasurer's office during office hours and inspect the affairs there for itself.[1] It therefore remains true that the real question of the control of the budget, so far as our states are concerned, is not one that has to do at all with the liberties and authority of the people—for in this nation that is forever settled—but one that is concerned with the more perfect administration of and the application of business principles in the business affairs of government. No sympathetic believer in our institutions will doubt that in the fulness of time a satisfactory solution of this question will be worked out.

[1] *Laws of Washington*, sec. 157.